HOW TO STUDY & LEARN

In this Series

How to Apply for a Job
How to Apply to an Industrial Tribunal
How to Be a Freelance Journalist
How to Be a Freelance Secretary
How to Be a Local Councillor
How to Be an Effective School Governor
How to Become an Au Pair
How to Buy & Run a Shop
How to Buy & Run a Small Hotel
How to Choose a Private School
How to Claim State Benefits
How to Communicate at Work
How to Conduct Staff Appraisals
How to Counsel People at Work
How to Do Voluntary Work Abroad
How to Do Your Own Advertising
How to Do Your Own PR
How to Emigrate
How to Employ & Manage Staff
How to Enjoy Retirement
How to Find Temporary Work Abroad
How to Get a Job Abroad
How to Get a Job in America
How to Get a Job in Australia
How to Get a Job in Europe
How to Get a Job in France
How to Get a Job in Germany
How to Get a Job in Hotels & Catering
How to Get a Job in Travel & Tourism
How to Get into Films & TV
How to Get into Radio
How to Get That Job
How to Help Your Child at School
How to Invest in Stocks & Shares
How to Keep Business Accounts
How to Know Your Rights at Work
How to Know Your Rights: Students
How to Know Your Rights: Teachers
How to Live & Work in America
How to Live & Work in Australia
How to Live & Work in Belgium
How to Live & Work in France
How to Live & Work in Germany
How to Live & Work in Hong Kong
How to Live & Work in Italy
How to Live & Work in Japan
How to Live & Work in New Zealand
How to Live & Work in Portugal
How to Live & Work in Saudi Arabia
How to Live & Work in Spain
How to Live & Work in the Gulf
How to Lose Weight & Keep Fit

How to Make a Wedding Speech
How to Manage a Sales Team
How to Manage Budgets & Cash Flows
How to Manage Computers at Work
How to Manage People at Work
How to Manage Your Career
How to Market Yourself
How to Master Book-Keeping
How to Master Business English
How to Master GCSE Accounts
How to Master Languages
How to Master Public Speaking
How to Pass Exams Without Anxiety
How to Pass That Interview
How to Plan a Wedding
How to Prepare Your Child for School
How to Publish a Book
How to Publish a Newsletter
How to Raise Business Finance
How to Raise Funds & Sponsorship
How to Rent & Buy Property in France
How to Rent & Buy Property in Italy
How to Retire Abroad
How to Return to Work
How to Run a Local Campaign
How to Run a Voluntary Group
How to Sell Your Business
How to Spend a Year Abroad
How to Start a Business from Home
How to Start a New Career
How to Start Your Own Business
How to Start Word Processing
How to Study Abroad
How to Study & Learn
How to Study & Live in Britain
How to Survive at College
How to Survive Divorce
How to Take Care of Your Heart
How to Teach Abroad
How to Travel Round the World
How to Understand Finance at Work
How to Use a Library
How to Work from Home
How to Work in an Office
How to Work with Dogs
How to Write a Press Release
How to Write a Report
How to Write an Assignment
How to Write an Essay
How to Write Business Letters
How to Write for Publication
How to Write for Television

Other titles in preparation

STUDY & LEARN

Your practical guide to effective study skills

Peter Marshall

How To Books

British Library Cataloguing in Publication Data
A catalogue record for this book is available from the British Library.

© Copyright 1995 by Peter Marshall.

First published in 1995 by How To Books Ltd, Plymbridge House,
Estover Road, Plymouth PL6 7PZ, United Kingdom.
Tel: (01752) 735251/695745. Fax: (01752) 695699. Telex: 45635.

Note: The material contained in this book is set out in good faith for general
guidance and no liability can be accepted for loss or expense incurred as a result of
relying in particular circumstances on statements made in the book. The laws and
regulations are complex and liable to change, and readers should check the current
position with the relevant authorities before making personal arrangements.

Typeset by PDQ Typesetting, Stoke-on-Trent
Printed and bound by The Cromwell Press, Broughton Gifford, Melksham,
Wiltshire.

Contents

Preface   7

1 **Getting your mind right**   9

Understanding yourself   9
Removing the barriers to success   14
Motivating yourself   19
Developing the will to learn   20
Adjusting the pressure   23
Developing good study habits   25
Using your mistakes   27
Summary   28
Case studies   29
Discussion points   30

2 **Organising yourself**   31

Planning realistically   31
Organising your system   37
Organising your time   41
Scheduling work, rest and play   46
Dealing with setbacks   47
Summary   49
Case studies   50
Discussion points   50

3 **Finding the information**   51

Assessing your study skills   51
Handling classes   51
Handling lectures   53
Handling group work   55
Using libraries   57
Developing your reading skills   60
Making notes   73

Summary 76
Case studies 78
Discussion points 79

4 **Developing your writing skills** 80

Functions of essays 80
Approaching the task 81
Writing the essay 82
Keeping to the word limit 86
Referencing your work 88
Making a final check 91
Summary 91
Case studies 92
Discussion points 93

5 **Developing your quantitative skills** 94

Checking your skills 94
Using symbols 95
Work fast – work accurately 95
Doing arithmetic 96
Dealing with averages 104
Graphs, charts and pictograms 105
Solving equations 110
Checklist for solving problems 111
Some final tips 113
Summary 113
Case studies 114
Discussion points 114

6 **Handling coursework and exams** 115

How you are assessed 115
Reaching your peak 118
Question spotting 119
Tutor-marked assignments 120
Computer-marked assignments 121
Final exam preparation 122
Handling the exam 126
Summary 132
Case studies 133
Discussion points 134

Further reading 135
Glossary 137
Index 141

Preface

Little, if anything, limits people's educational achievement more than their own self doubts. Pupils of all ages point to high flyers and say: 'Oh, he's just naturally bright; he doesn't even have to try.' This is what I call the 'fallacy of the naturally successful'. It is technique which, in the main, determines success. Look closely and you'll see that pupil's techniques are better.

Then there is the 'fallacy of achievement and ability'. Most adults assume that their achievement level on leaving school reflected their ability; if they didn't achieve it was because they were simply not clever enough. The low expectations of those around them after that served to reinforce such self-doubt. But it simply isn't true. A whole host of influences besides natural ability helped to determine their school performance.

We may not be able to increase the grey matter we were born with, but we can do a lot to improve the way it works. Look at it this way. The mind is like a computer. Here, the hardware determines its absolute power, but the software determines how effectively the computer is used. Our brains are our computers and our knowledge and skills are our software. Just as we can improve the computer's capacity by improving the programming, so we can improve our brain's capacity in the same way. This book aims to show you how to begin doing this.

Designed for all age groups, its aims are to help you break through the barriers to achievement which slow so many down – the 'fallacy of slow and careful reading', for example, and the 'fallacy of practice'. It will show you how to shift into a higher gear in your reading and writing, how to develop skill and confidence in handling quantitative material, and how to supercharge your performance by enlightened self-knowledge and effective organisation.

Peter Marshall

Is this you?

GCSE student   A level student

College student

Undergraduate   Research student

Postgraduate

Studying humanities   Studying science/technology

Studying a professional subject

Distance learner   Examination candidate

Reviser

Essay writer   Doing a project

Preparing a dissertation

Mature student   Exam re-taker

Diploma student

Applying for a place   Applying for a scholarship

Foreign student

Teacher   Lecturer

Tutor

Student counsellor   Librarian

1
Getting Your Mind Right

UNDERSTANDING YOURSELF

Before you can know the best direction to take and how to get to where you want to go, you need to assess where you're starting from:

- what type of person you are
- what your strengths and weaknesses are
- what your thinking style is
- how you learn best.

Many people feel vaguely dissatisfied with their level of achievement, while not really knowing what they want to do in life. Their thoughts about the subject just swirl around and no progress is made. They wake up one morning and realise they have grown old, and regret that they have wasted so much of their lives. You've got to crystallise those thoughts, that is to make them stand still so that they can be assessed and a starting point found.

Making a self-assessment
Putting your thoughts down on paper is a good way of doing this. Using someone else as a sounding-board is another. Since we often hold inappropriate beliefs about ourselves, for all sorts of ego-defensive reasons, your assessment needs to be objective, based on some set of rules. The following tests will help you begin to understand which direction in life is right for you.

Test your ideas about a career
Suppose one of your family had an idea for a new product that would benefit almost everyone, and wanted you to become involved. In which three of the following ways would you most prefer to be involved?

A. Design the system for producing it. _____

B. Plan and control the financial side of the business. _____

C. Teach user-courses in schools and colleges. _____

D. Write press articles about it. _____

E. Manage a retail outlet for the product. _____

F. Design a marketable product, plus its packaging, from the basic idea. _____

G. Train the workers. _____

H. Find ways of maximising profit. _____

I. Supervise the production. _____

J. Sell the product. _____

K. Be involved in building, fitting-out and tooling up the factory premises. _____

L. Improve the production system by computerisation and automation. _____

M. Set up the company and employ your inventor-relative. _____

N. Set up an agency of your own, where the public could use the product (without buying it) at a cost. _____

O. Be involved 'hands on' in building the product. _____

P. Market the product overseas. _____

Q. Become knowledgeable in every aspect of the business and so earn a place at the top. _____

R. Be Personnel Officer to the firm. _____

Now check your answers against those in box 1 below to assess what could be the right direction in life for you. This is not a definitive test, but it should help you begin to look at the issues in a constructive way.

Box 1. *Interpreting occupational predispositions test*

K, L, O – Practical work.
B, E, I – Managerial, financial, administrative.
C, G, R – Social professions, teaching.
A, D, F – Creative.
H, M, Q – Competitive occupations.
J, N, P – Occupations which give you some independence of action, excitement and adventure.

Unfounded beliefs about ourselves can often dominate our thinking if we let them. These are beliefs influenced by emotions, prejudices and an over-reliance on past experiences. If you don't agree with any of the outcomes of this test, you need to be sure that your reasons are rational and not rooted in these false beliefs.

Test your ideas about courses

Now try this test.

1. Without thinking about it, jot down the first 20 educational course subjects which come into your head, regardless of whether you like them or not.

2. Now, again without thinking about it, jot down two desirable things about each.

3. Lastly, try to analyse the list of desirable qualities into common themes. This will give you a more objective idea of what would motivate you in a course and help you to choose what is appropriate for you to study.

Test your thinking style

People tend to have different 'hemispherical biases'. That is, they differ in how much they use the left side of their brains (language, or sequential processor) compared with the right side (gestalt, or spatial processor).

Try Coltheart's test: think through the alphabet and mentally count the number of letters with a curve in them. Write down your answer. Now go through the alphabet again mentally counting those which have an 'ee' sound in them. Write down your answer. Now go to box 2, below, to interpret your answers.

Of course, no occupation utilises only one kind of ability. With a few exceptions nobody's brain involves one side only; these are *relative* differences.

Box 2. *Interpreting Coltheart test results*

There are 11 letters with a curve in them and 11 with an 'ee' sound. Missing one letter on either sub-test could be due to chance, but a score of 9 or less on the curves sub-test suggests you are relatively left-brain dominant; a score of 9 or less on the 'ee' sounds sub-test suggests you are more right-brain dominant than most. An equal score on both tests is unusual, but would suggest you are relatively even-brained.

All subjects relate more or less well to particular hemispherical biases. Some require more left-brain ability and some more right-brain ability. Some favour more even-brained development. It would be impossible to list all the thousands of occupations in life and relate them to the thinking styles they favour.

To give you some idea, though, subjects which require **sequential** thinking – like computer programming, bookmaking, book-keeping, analytical statistics and a variety of problem-solving jobs – require relatively left-brain abilities. Subjects which require more **spatial** ability, like accountancy, management, art and design, architecture and air-piloting require more right-brain styles of thinking.

If you understand your own thinking style you can use the best methods of studying your subject, too. Maths, for example is usually regarded as a predominantly right-brain ability, but the mathematical-ability theorist, Poincaré, identified both right-brain and left-brain styles of coping with the subject.

Similarly, with adult literacy teachers: a word-building approach will work best in the early stages for relatively left-brain dominant pupils, while a flash card method will work best for relatively right-brained dominant ones.

Ability levels
Which of the following do you honestly think applies to your intelligence level?

dull   _____
below average   _____
average   _____
above average   _____
bright   _____
gifted   _____

Children are pretty good judges of their own ability levels. Adults may be less so, because their self-conceptions have often been subjected to a downward modifying force. By the time we leave compulsory schooling we have been socialised into believing that our academic achievement level at 16 or 18 reflects our ability. Not so! There are all sorts of factors which act on us to restrict our achievement at school.

Research has shown that home and family background influences play an enormous part. The money available, the conditions, the attitudes of parents, brothers and sisters towards education, the examples they set and the amount of interest in, and help they give to a child's effort all contribute significantly to the way his or her education turns out.

- Some children are too small or too quiet to be noticed, and those who aren't noticed are not expected to do well by teachers. Teacher expectations are a major influence on educational achievement level, often more so than high ability.

- Some children lack a competitive spirit, or do not really know what educational effort is for.

- The behaviour and attitude towards educational achievement among friends at school and away from school also has a powerful effect.

- Then there were all kinds of personal things that had nothing to do with ability level – competing interests, courting, emotional problems and so on.

Your achievement level when you left school reflected far more than whether you had the 'grey matter' or not.

Look at the famous late-developers in history. The physicist Albert Einstein left school at 15 with no qualifications. The composer Richard Wagner was a late-developer, teaching himself music as a teenager. Ludwig van Beethoven was more or less written off by his teacher, and so was the naturalist Charles Darwin. Julius Caesar did little with his life until he was approaching middle-age and Frederick the Great of Prussia achieved little until late in life.

Task commitment and creativity

What matters more is 'task commitment' and 'creativity'. It is the presence of the three elements at once – intelligence, creativity and task commitment – that tends to produce great works. However, people with brilliantly high levels of intelligence very often lack the other two. Robert Sternberg, Professor of Psychology at Yale University, argued that very high intelligence often leads to rigidity of thinking. This could explain the lack of creativity often found among such individuals. If you have an IQ of between 100 and 120 you've got all you need to do most things in life.

Furthermore, IQ can be boosted to some degree. Most experts agree that only about 80 per cent of our IQ is genetically endowed. That part you can't change; but you *can* work on the other part. It is very unlikely that your learning potential has been developed anywhere near to capacity.

Being in control

You're in control now, though, but you must have the courage to realise it. Most of the doubts we have about our ability to progress are really unfounded.

REMOVING THE BARRIERS TO SUCCESS

I can't keep up – I've always been a plodder

It's probably only a lack of confidence that is keeping you slow – frightened that you'll miss something out. But there's a link between speed of processing and difficulty. All 'difficulty' is really at the processing level, *ie* the time it takes to solve a problem.

Intelligence theory suggests that our brain is a one-channel processor. The information in it is eroded by three things – 'trace-decay', 'interference from other thoughts' and 'overload' (when too much information is being dealt with, signals disappear). When such erosion exceeds a certain point the process collapses. We would describe the experience by saying, 'The problem was too difficult'.

Just consider how you would stop a roadway, or any other channel, from becoming overloaded, or congested, though. You would just speed up the flow. Well, the same applies in our heads. The quicker the information is dealt with, the less it decays and the less it is affected by other thoughts. In a nutshell the faster you deal with something the easier it is.

But this is a rational analysis and, as pointed out earlier, it tends to be the irrational beliefs which dominate our thinking, beliefs like 'By working more slowly we'll avoid mistakes'. That is, unless we make a conscious effort to reject the irrational in favour of the rational – the scientifically based knowledge that accuracy comes with speed. Better to do it quickly and run over it again than do it slowly once. When you have overcome this confidence hurdle enormous strides can be made. It's quite feasible to double your reading speed in six weeks, for example.

I've got no staying power

'I start out with all the enthusiasm in the world and then it dries up.' Very often this is because we cannot positively evaluate postponement of gratification to achieve long-term goals or, in plain English, we can't see further than our nose.

Again, this is a learned response. Some people are more aware than others of the value of delaying earnings and having fun while they work hard for qualifications. They see clearly that the reward at the end will be so much greater than if they take what pleasure is available now. It's like investing your money instead of spending it; you know you will receive greater benefit from your earnings during your life-time if you do so. You will get the benefit of your earnings plus interest.

This kind of value is learned from our home-background. That's where values start. If academic values were important in your family, you will have developed those values, too. If your parents did not, and often could not, afford to postpone their earnings so that they could go to college, then you will not have found that value easy to accept.

This is a necessary value to develop, though. If you're really going to learn you've got to make sacrifices. You can't be out and about every night and studying at evening classes at the same time. You can't be earning a full-time salary when you're in full-time education. You can't have your cake and eat it too. You may well, by now, have seen for yourself the value of postponing pleasure and earnings for long-term rewards. Some of your friends and neighbours will now be driving better cars, living in better houses and working in more interesting careers because they did so.

You are now in charge.

• What you didn't learn as a child you can learn now.

Look around you, see the real value of education. Teach yourself in adulthood the educational values that you did not pick up as a child.

I'm afraid of speaking out in class

Many of us fear appearing silly if we speak out. Testing your ideas on others, especially the teacher, is crucial to learning and your achievement will suffer if you are not prepared to do so. Get over your shyness. Yes, it's embarrassing to have your view rejected if it goes against the grain. The crowd-view is often wrong, though.

A checklist of study skills

How good are *you* at –

Planning your studies

Managing setbacks

Skim reading

Using libraries

Reading texts

Note-taking

Summarising

Prioritising

Essay planning

Referencing

Keeping to word limits

Keeping to the point

Writing skills

Error-checking

Using statistics

Using symbols

Using illustrations

Preparing coursework

Seeking advice

Weighing evidence

Arguing a case

Working alone

Working in a group

Question spotting

Scanning

Managing exam nerves

Logical thinking

Close reading

Spelling

Punctuation

Creative thinking

Retaining information

Grammar

Staying the course

Learning from experience

It's often based on taken-for-granted knowledge, rather than rational thinking. If your own view is based on rational arguments it is likely to be superior. That doesn't mean other people will accept it; attitudes are very hard to change, but that's their loss, not yours.

Game playing
Continued educational failure can be due to 'game playing'. Are you walking in the gutter to avoid falling into it?

Aiming low
Many people play self-destructive games, without realising it. When people play this one they invariably have a low level of self-esteem. They have known all their life that they have achieved less than their true potential. They have probably had friends and relatives – not to mention teachers – who have never tired of telling them so. What childhood is all about, though, is learning how to cope with life as an adult. If the only thing they learned was how to cope with low self-esteem, they will tend to maintain that psychological state throughout their life. After all, they don't know how to cope with success. How could they?

The desire to lose
Perpetual losing is not always due to low self-esteem, though. Some perpetual losers have a high level of self-esteem. They may have difficulty coping with uncertainty. You can never guarantee success, but you can guarantee failure, so they predict it and make their prophecy come true. Perpetual losers subconsciously find ways of ensuring they fail.

If a perpetual loser has a high level of self-esteem, he tends to blame others, the system or fate, for his failures. If he has a low level of self-esteem he blames himself. This way both types protect the level of self-esteem they have learned to live with. Research has shown that females are more likely to blame themselves for underachievement; males tend to blame forces outside themselves.

One of the most noticeable ways perpetual losers ensure their own failure is by setting goals that are either too high, so that they have to fail, or too low, so that if they succeed it is nothing to write home about.

The good news is that we are all capable of changing ourselves. We must first accept the truth about our natures, though. Remember, too, such truth is easily obscured by irrational beliefs. If you recognise yourself in the above paragraphs start setting realistic goals, and have the courage to risk both 'failure' and 'success'. Don't waste time and energy blaming others when things go wrong; your life is in your own hands. Start learning what it's like to be successful, from the first, uncomfortable days to the ultimate feelings of fulfilment and mastery of your own destiny.

I suffer mental fatigue if I study too long

It may surprise you to know that physiologically there is no such thing as 'mental fatigue'. Fatigue applies only to muscles. It happens when their waste products begin to poison them, because they can't dispose of them quick enough. The feeling of tiredness makes the body slow down, until the muscle system can cope with such waste products. The brain has no muscles, though, so this can't happen.

Furthermore, when muscles get tired they start to lose accuracy of operation. Try playing the piano or typing immediately after a weight training session, and see how accurate you are. Where extreme brain exertion is concerned, though, tests have shown that no loss of accuracy need occur.

What does cause loss of accuracy in such circumstances is boredom from the repetitive mental effort and the distracting effects of bodily discomfort – from muscle fatigue. Sitting too long in one position – especially a hunched and unnatural one – puts strain on the neck and the back. Those prone to indigestion and stomach disorders will suffer in that region, too. Eyes also begin to tire. The mixture of all these things is what people mistake as mental fatigue and these effects can be avoided. Sit in a comfortable chair with the back straight; if possible have your table top slight raised towards you. Use plenty of light. Don't sit for too long, get up and walk around now and again.

That's not to say the mind can go on at any level of pressure. Cognitive breakdown can occur. This is a sudden collapse of a problem-solving process in the brain. The point at which this occurs determines which test questions we can answer and which we cannot. Cognitive breakdown arises from channel-overload, trace-decay, and interference from other thoughts – not from duration of attention. The mind works best when physical effort is at minimum level. Have you noticed how clear, and how energetic your thinking is in the dead of night when you are unable to sleep? have you noticed how the more you think, the harder it is to drift-off? If fatigue followed mental effort this would not be the case.

It's specially difficult for me because...

'I have serious motor-control disorder, I'm blind, I'm deaf, I'm this, I'm that...' The writer once saw a dog run over; its hips were broken. The owner didn't have it put down, but asked the vet to inject it with steroids and pain killers and put it to bed in its basket. Before long, to everyone's amazement, the dog was walking around, but with both hind legs in the air, walking on its front paws only. Animals don't whinge, they get on with things as best they can. Each of us has to use what we've got, not mourn that we haven't. Look at what Helen Keller achieved – as a scholar, author and social reformer – despite being blind and deaf. Look what Stephen Hawking has achieved – probing the origins of the universe – despite having crippling motor neurone disease. You can't change your biological nature, but you can do a lot with what you have got intact.

MOTIVATING YOURSELF

What motivates people to learn has been the subject of much research. The philosopher William James defined our prime motivating force as the desire to harmonise our discrepant selves. He saw different micro-level selves that make up our whole psyche, things like 'actual self-concept' and 'ideal self-concept'. In plain English, these mean 'what I am' and 'what I think I ought to be'. If there is little difference between these then you are really pretty satisfied with yourself; you are not motivated to change. If you want to motivate yourself you have to create dissatisfaction.

It may be, however, that you are dissatisfied, but you really can't see yourself ever achieving what you desire. Sometimes a kind of 'learned hopelessness' sets in. This may be because you did not have an appropriate role-model as a child – there was no-one occupying the role in life that you, yourself, now wish to occupy. When children reach adulthood, however, they can take charge of their own destinies.

You need to imagine yourself in the desired role before you can get there. Look around you at others who occupy the role you desire to be in. Ask yourself whether, putting all rational doubts about yourself aside, there is really any reason at all why you cannot be like them? If there are not, then make those people your role-models.

Motivation requires dissatisfaction

If you're an under achiever who has got used to his lot, or a high achiever who feels he is at his pinnacle, you've got to cultivate the dissatisfaction in yourself. Never accept that you've reached the limit of your development. Even what are often thought to be 'gifts' can be improved with practice. It is estimated that people can improve by 25% to 40% in most areas.

Getting more knowledge for less effort

Learning doesn't simply mean increasing your knowledge. It means finding ways of doing the same but with less effort. Here you have an important secret of motivation. Approach learning in this way and you will have turned what demotivates most people (the prospect of all that effort) into a motivator (the prospect of less of all that effort). Research shows that the highest achievers actually spend less time on study than those who achieve at more modest levels.

But surely balanced people should be satisfied?

Think about it. Dissatisfaction is the very stuff of life. A gap between what you have and what you need is what keeps you going. Even in your very breathing process, it's only because your body craves more oxygen than it has at any moment that you keep breathing. If it ever becomes satisfied with what it has got it dies. Dissatisfaction, motivation, is life itself – is living unnatural? Those who are most dissatisfied are those with a zest for life; it's the same thing.

DEVELOPING THE WILL TO LEARN

How often is it said that if you want to achieve something enough you'll achieve it. It isn't true. To achieve something you have to *will* it, too.

What's the difference between wishing and willing something? A wish is passive, like putting your tooth under the pillow. 'Willing' is active. In today's world you've got to *make* things happen.

To learn successfully you have to develop a will to learn. This involves analysing what you've got going for you, and what your weaknesses are. Devoting yourself to a serious quest for ways of improving your learning is not the same thing as ways of increasing your knowledge. You have to 'learn to learn'. Many highly intelligent people never do this, because, in their early years of education, they got by with intuition, whereas most have to develop skills. Later on, though, when those skills are necessary, when their intuition won't suffice for the more complex problems, the highly intelligent ones very often lose out; they've never 'learned how to learn'. Consequently, they become alienated to school, blame the curriculum, say it's too slow for them and settle into a life of low achievement. The 'will to learn' is the key to high learning achievements, and the 'will to learn' shares a bed with dissatisfaction.

Practice doesn't necessarily make perfect

The old saying that 'practice makes perfect' is misleading. In fact, a too ready reliance on practice is more likely to ensure imperfection. Let us see why.

Repetition is not the best way of learning for it can lead to 'practice error'. Does continuous walking make someone a more skilled walker? Does repeated driving make someone a better driver? Think about it! No, it usually makes them a worse one. Does increased handwriting make someone a better handwriter? Those who write most often tend to have the worst handwriting.

We all tend to make more errors and ineffective actions than accurate and effective actions; if we learned by repetition we would all deteriorate in all of our abilities.

Furthermore, if repetition were the source of learning, then we would only be able to apply our learning to identical sets of circumstances to those in which we practised.

In the early stages of learning something, we err more than we succeed; yet it is in this phase that most learning takes place. It can't be the repetition that's teaching us.

Don't practise – experiment

Always vary your procedures. You can then discover which is best. Find different approaches. Do more thinking than acting. Analyse what you are going to do before you do it, and afterwards review it. Your goal should be not simply to achieve an error-free result but to become familiar with the conditions and behaviour which bring it about. You are educating your 'will to learn', making it a more and more formidable force. Learn to recognise success, how you achieved it and what it feels like.

Be competitive

Competition is a powerful motivator. Compare yourself with

others. Try to learn the secrets of your most successful colleagues. The champions do it. You'll often see boxers in the audience at a big fight. Challenge yourself regularly, too; use your creative powers to design new tests for yourself.

Develop good study habits
We are creatures of habit so we might as well use this trait to good advantage. Develop good study habits and actively discard those you know to be bad ones.

Break through plateaux
Have you noticed how learning tends to plateau? You get so far and then your progress sticks. It is not necessarily that your desire and determination have dried up. It is more likely that the methods you used to reach your present level are not appropriate for surpassing it. New techniques must be devised, and you have to find them.

Start experimenting again to find a technique which will bring you further. Here are some suggestions to help you find a way forward.

- Try planning and preparing in great detail.

- Try without any preparation at all.

- Work intensively for a period.

- Work in a casual way for a period.

- Vary your speeds of work.

- Work at different times of the day.

The art of persistent hesitation
Our knowledge gels into rigid structures if we let it. We only continue to learn whilst those structures retain some flexibility. To prolong our ability to learn, whether we are talking about a particular subject or about 'learnability' in life generally, we must resist early fixations of ideas.

Always look for different solutions, using the whole range of your experience. Interact with your knowledge, by looking for possible objections. Use these as starting points for further exploration, designing defences to your view or looking for other solutions which these objections suggest.

You should aim for not only extensive knowledge, but also fine tuning of operation in using it. When you feel you have gained a mastery of something test your proficiency on others. Discuss the knowledge you've learned, welcome criticism, though distinguish the constructive from the destructive kinds and ignore the latter. Constructive criticism will contain defensible argument, destructive criticism will not.

Discouragement is always in plentiful supply. It is a common social trait. If one member of a group aspires to greater achievement than the others, the crowd will discourage him – 'Don't be daft, you can't do that'. This is because a shared worldview and a common achievement level is important for the group-member's emotional security. If anyone rocks the boat it shows up the inadequacies of the rest.

Using your subconscious

Your mind does not stop learning when you finish for the day. It is said that the point of highest recall of material studied is not until 10 minutes afterwards. Some researchers have shown that people remember things better days afterwards, than immediately afterwards.

We may also remember uncompleted tasks better than completed ones. If we learn something and then give up, we'll 'put it to the back of our mind'. But if we learn something we know we are going to come back to, our subconscious takes over and continues to think about it. If you've ever tried to learn to play a musical instrument and given up once or twice for reasonably long periods, you will be familiar with a sense of surprise at how much more proficient you seemed to be each time you re-started than you were when you left off last time. This 'benefit of recess' is one of the reasons why study periods should be kept relatively short and spaced out. It gives your subconscious a chance to do some of the work.

ADJUSTING THE PRESSURE

Make your early learning endeavours as easy and anxiety-free as you can.

• Don't be too concerned about speed.

• Don't be too preoccupied with avoiding errors.

- Whatever you do don't try to master great chunks of the subject all at once. Take nibbles, not bites.

- In the early stages you should not plan your learning in terms of set periods of study either, but rather in terms of the achievement of 'learning objectives'.

It is not being able to perform a task, or regurgitate knowledge error-free that amounts to learning. It is knowing what it feels like to do so that is the learning itself. This is why it is important to work towards mastering small bits of the knowledge or process in the early stages. Your mind and body get a proper chance to familiarise themselves with the whole of the process.

When you can perform the skill or regurgitate knowledge error-free practice becomes useful in serving to rigidify the structures (though tentatively where factual knowledge is concerned). However, it is quality of practice which is important, not quantity. If you aim for quantity of practice, eg number of repetitions, or a set period of practice, you are more likely to cement your errors. Shorter periods of practice, frequently analysed, will help prevent this happening.

Learning a skill or learning to use knowledge is rather like building a machine. Imagine you're building or modifying an engine. You can't put too much pressure on it at first as it will break down, but as you gradually tune it towards perfection you can put your foot down harder and harder.

Modifying your mind is the same. This is, indeed, what you're doing when you're learning a skill or learning to use knowledge; you are making, or programming new brain circuitry. When the system is only beginning to take shape you can't put much pressure on it or the process you are carrying out will break down (cognitive breakdown). The less streamlined the system you've made, the less intact the circuitry. The more leaps and jugglings have to be made with the information to achieve the desired result, (eg solve a problem or carry out a task). You reach a point of channel-overload. There is just too much going on in your head. You become confused and have to admit defeat.

However, as the circuitry becomes more streamlined, as each gap becomes plugged with a learned, intuitively usable sub-routine, more and more channel-capacity becomes available for data handling. Consequently, the more the skill is learned the more pressure you can put on it. In fact, in the final stages of completion, pressure acts to reinforce the connections in the system.

In the early stages cognitive breakdown thresholds are low. They become higher as skill develops. Go for small objectives at first, but as completion begins to take place start going for distance and speed, so to speak.

When you feel you have begun to master the skill or the ability to use knowledge complete the process by deliberately putting obstacles in your way. Make yourself recall material or carry out a learned process while various distractions are taking place (loud music, chatter). Put yourself into all kinds of unfavourable conditions while you apply the new knowledge to different problems or perform the new skill. Teachers used to ask pupils to say their tables backwards to complete the learning process. This is, indeed, performing the skill under unfavourable conditions.

Similarly, it will help you complete the learning of a poem, a speech, a script and many other things if you ask a friend to read a newspaper aloud while you recite the material. If you can do so under such unfavourable conditions the programming of your neural circuitry will have become quite rigidly established. Common sources of interference have themselves become associated with the stored sequence so that they do not necessarily distract you. When you can recall knowledge or carry out a skill in such distracting circumstances you will have reached a new superheight of proficiency. If you can do it when circumstances are abnormal you can be pretty sure of doing it when they are not.

DEVELOPING GOOD STUDY HABITS

Controlling each part

Experts always seem to do things more quickly than novices. In fact, they're doing them *differently* (although the differences are too subtle to be noticed). It is controls built into their techniques, learned by trial and error, to prevent failure at various points, which make the expert's performance different from the novice's. The beginner has not yet learned where these controls are required. Consider the expert waiter who can carry four or more plates while a novice would come to grief with only three. The waiter has learned by trial and error all of the weakest positions and most vulnerable movements; he has also learned how to avoid and correct balancing crises.

It is ease of operation that characterises proficiency and ease is achieved through control. When you can't quite master a skill you have to take it to bits to find out why. You will find the bit that needs controlling if you look hard enough.

Seeking out general principles

General principles remain constant, but applications vary. Only when you have looked at many different applications can you really say you have a grasp of the general principles.

- Relate your learning to your interests.

- Aim to develop as wide an experience in your chosen field as possible.

- Formulate your arguments in different styles.

- Reformulate them to apply them to imaginary problems, too.

Consolidating your gains

Tell people what you've learned. Discuss it with them at length. All their responses, verbal and non-verbal, and everything you do to help them understand the message, will become associated in your memory with the material you have learned. This will consolidate your learning and make it easier for you to recall. The more people you talk to about it the better your consolidation and recall potential will be.

Many of the people you meet will have taken the same courses as you. Many would be only too glad to talk about the subjects even though years may have elapsed since they studied them. Their exam questions will have been different, but this is all to the good.

Real understanding and learning

You cannot say you really understand an argument until you've considered all its strengths and weaknesses and you can only say you've really learned a piece of knowledge when you've related it to other knowledge.

Being an active learner

Don't just sit there and listen to the information being dished out by a teacher or advice by a friend. Always interact. That's how understanding is achieved. If the information you are receiving is verbal, ask questions. If you are reading it from a book or journal set yourself quizzes and change the conditions, posing 'What ifs'.

Reflecting on your work

Think about the skills you are learning during odd moments. Waiting times are ideal for this, eg waiting for trains or buses, waiting in dental surgeries, or waiting for friends. They are (hopefully) rather short intervals and there is nothing else to do. Your mind is looking for something to occupy it.

You can commit facts quickly to memory using **mnemonics** (memory tricks dealt with in a later chapter) so that you can mentally recall them at such moments and play around with them. Thinking between learning sessions is highly valuable, but most people do not realise it and, if they do, they don't use it.

Cramming

It's not advisable to rely on cramming as a learning technique. It doesn't work well. It leaves little time for mental association of material, so that fewer neural connections are made.

USING YOUR MISTAKES

> The road to wisdom?
> Well its plain
> And simple to express:
> Err and err and err again,
> But less and less and less.
> (Piet Hein)

Don't live in horror of mistakes. It's not the error which you should seek to avoid but the practice which brought it about. Indeed, if you maintain an experimental attitude, essential for effective learning, mistakes are inevitable.

It is persistent errors that you should be on the look out for. There are certain areas where these are more likely than others; an obvious example is in spelling. People often have their own personal persistent errors in things like multiplication tables, too. Persistent errors can affect you in learning any knowledge or skill. If they arise you must take the process of learning to bits and analyse why it's happening.

Lastly, take responsibility for your own failings. Don't blame others for your errors. Nobody will take you seriously. Worse, it will ensure that you never learn, because you only learn by correcting for mistakes and weaknesses. To do this you have to admit them first to yourself.

Blaming others can be a symptom of, or the start of, a life-long tendency towards destructive game-playing. It protects your self-esteem even if you fail, and fear of damage to the self-esteem is one of the things that spurs us on to success. It will, therefore, relieve you of the need ever to achieve highly and gain you a bit of short-term sympathy. But deal with situations in this manner and you may lose (or never develop) the ability to cope in any other way. Perpetual failing may become a way of life.

To be an achiever in life, you must accept that errors are necessary to the learning process, but try to avoid too much familiarity with what it's like to fail. The road you want to feel most comfortable on is that which leads to success.

SUMMARY

1. Get to know yourself.

2. Imagine yourself where you want to be.

3. Don't put obstacles in your way.

4. Look for general principles.

5. Don't push too hard at first, but put yourself under pressure as you approach proficiency.

6. Never accept that you've reached the limit of your development.

7. Working fast improves accuracy.

8. Practice doesn't necessarily make perfect.

9. Compete with yourself and others.

10. Separate constructive from destructive criticism.

11. When you reach plateaux you need new methods to get past them.

12. Use your subconscious.

13. Use your mistakes.

14. Consolidate your gains by reflecting between study periods and discussing what you've learned with others.

CASE STUDIES

Tom sits back

Tom Elliot is a pretty typical student. He has just entered university, after completing his A levels in sixth form. Ask him what he wants to do after he graduates and he'll tell you he hasn't a clue. He is not looking that far ahead. Tom expects to still be spoonfed, like he was in sixth form. He's going to get a shock when it dawns on him that it's largely down to him to discover things for himself now he's at university.

Tom is not really a flyer, he's a qualifier. He feels that as long as he attends all the classes and does all his essays more or less on time and revises adequately at the end of the course he'll come out with a 2:2.

Jennifer is in control

Jennifer Goss is an exceptional student. She is 23 years old and is taking a diploma in management studies, after which she intends to go on to university to take a BA. She intends to pursue a career in business management.

She reads fast and efficiently. She thrives on competition with others and she is constantly competing with herself, too. She is not thrown off balance by spiteful criticism; when criticism is constructive she welcomes it. She is highly serious about her learning and takes every opportunity to practise her knowledge in the company of others with similar interests.

Karen: too late to catch up?

Karen Morris left school believing without question that her lack of any qualifications reflected her lack of ability to attain any. She became an office junior and learned to type, file and deal with correspondence. She is dissatisfied with her job and over the years it has made her rather frustrated and grumpy. However, she would never try to picture herself in any other role. 'Oh, it's too late now!', she would say to friends. 'I'm thirty-five; you can't change course at this stage in life.'

Karen took up a night-school class in French, because she has friends from Grenoble staying with her each year. She also visits them in France. She is unable to depart from the rote learning methods which she has always used. She also seems quite unable to let go of her belief that reading slowly is reading accurately, fearing that if she speeds up she will miss something.

DISCUSSION POINTS

1. Are you putting obstacles in the way of your own success? Is anyone you know doing the same?

2. What career do you think you are most suited for? How far is it what you would like? Can you imagine yourself in such a position? If not, why not?

3. Consider some of the ways new methods could help you get past learning plateaux.

2
Organising Yourself

To organise means to give structure to your endeavours, making arrangements in advance to help things run smoothly and lead to the outcome you want. It is to programme, as far as is possible, all the lights to green.

PLANNING REALISTICALLY

When making plans it is easy to expect too much of yourself. We all do it. Planning realistically is harder; it means accepting the truth that we are not as perfect as we would like to think. Conversely, some people tend to underestimate their abilities.

To plan realistically we must look objectively at the evidence of our capabilities and our tendencies. Yes, we may be quite capable of working at that rate but, in practice, do we do so? Do we resist the temptations to daydream, to sit in the sun, to join friends for a drink?

'Ah yes,' you might say, 'but all that's a thing of the past. Where this course is concerned I'm not going to let anything get in the way of my plans.'

How do you know that? If you could be tempted before, what evidence do you have that you will not 'bunk off' again? You can't tell until the time comes. The best evidence you have of how you respond to such situations is what you did in the past. Everyone who gives up smoking is quite determined that they will not start again, but almost all of them do. What you decide when you are in one mood or situation, may not hold true when your mood or situation changes.

Coping with the unexpected
Then there are the 'unknowns'. We never know what lies around the corner. We get colds and flu now and again, but cannot plan when we are going to get them in advance, nor how many times they will occur.

You need to take all these things into account to plan realistically. Your rate of progress will not be the same as that which you could achieve if all the circumstances remained ideal. You have to knock a bit off to allow for the unforeseen and for natural human weakness.

Contingency planning
Even the best laid plans go wrong at times, but successful people have other cards up their sleeves – they make *contingency plans*.

Basing plans on information
An essential component of planning is information. Your ability to achieve a particular work-rate depends partly on what time of day you work. Not all periods will be equally productive for you.

Planning must also take account of a number of time-scales. When you have made your plan, consider its weak points and make a proverbial 'Plan B' to get you through if these links fail.

ORGANISING YOUR ENVIRONMENT

The way you arrange your place of study will have a good or bad effect on the progress you make. Consider such things as

- space
- heat
- light
- freedom from noise and interruption
- comfortable seating.

Planning your space
Study is a private affair. You can't grapple with new ideas while others are watching television or chatting about their holidays in the same room.

If you have a study in your house, where you can work undisturbed in peace, you are very fortunate. For most it's the bedroom, but many don't have sole use of that either; brothers and sisters use it too.

Adult learners
Adult learners with young children at home have particular problems here. When exams are getting close it might even be a good idea to move out for a couple of weeks and stay in a guest

house or a friend or relative's house if peace during the day and undisturbed sleep at night is unlikely.

Using a library
Where no facilities for undisturbed periods of study are available, don't try to make do in a room where other things are going on. Instead, check whether private study rooms are available at your school or college. If not, the college or town library is your next best bet. Libraries have reading tables and college libraries sometimes have private study cubicles which can be booked at the desk. At least it should be quiet in libraries and if people are making a noise you can ask the librarian to request quiet.

Your own space
Supposing you do have your own space, either study or bedroom; the effectiveness of your study will depend in part on how you organise it. *Ergonomists* (experts in efficiency of action within environments) propose a *work triangle'*. This means arranging those facilities you use most so that you can reach them all easily – without moving from your seat, or at least without walking more than a couple of steps.

- Among your books it is likely to be dictionaries, thesaurus and handbooks that you will use most, so position them closest to you.

- Your pens, highlighters, correcting fluid, stapler and so on should be within reach from your chair; various low-priced 'desk tidies' are available for the purpose.

- Your course notes need to be near at hand as does a supply of scrap paper.

- If you have a computer, word processor or typewriter place it where you can operate it with least strain on the wrists, eyes and other body parts; this will be dealt with later under the heading of 'comfort'.

Arranging your space is one thing but for maximum efficiency other things have to be attended to as well, like heat, light and noise.

The right temperature
You can't grapple with complex ideas if the heat is making you fall

asleep. People differ as to the room temperature they prefer. But remember, you are not in the room to relax after a hard day's work, so the ideal temperature will be lower than that in which the other members of the family are watching the television. A reasonable temperature for people when studying is around 15.5 degrees celsius (60 degrees fahrenheit). The type of heater used is also important. Electric fires produce their heating effect directly onto surfaces, such as the skin, without heating the surrounding air very much. Fan heaters, however, heat the air and blow it around; but warm air is not only sleep-inducing, it is also dust-laden. It's not very healthy to breathe for long periods.

Using computers
If you are using a computer the problems will be magnified. Most computers have their own fans to keep the unit cool and they throw out dust, too. Added to this the electromagnetic field collects the dust towards the screen and then fires it directly into the user's face for him or her to inhale in concentrated form. It is also said to cause skin and eye irritation. More will be said about VDU screens later.

The right lighting
Light is important to prevent eye strain (which as explained in chapter 1 is partly what people wrongly think is 'mental fatigue'). We know that light affects our moods and levels of alertness. The light falling on the retina starts a process of signal relays which causes the pineal gland, deep inside the brain, to secrete a hormone called melatonin. This is picked up by the hypothalamus which responds by making the body ready for sleep.

Striplighting may give a bright, daylight effect, but it can cause headaches in some people, because of its flicker. The best kind of lighting is daylight, through a window. Extra 'focused' light from a reading lamp is useful and students are advised to include this relatively inexpensive item in their equipment list.

Daylight is not always the best light source. If you are using a computer or word processor, sunlight can produce glare on the screen, and it is this glare which causes many of the headaches that users suffer. Glare can be caused by artificial lights, too. Anti-glare screen filters can be fitted over your screen to alleviate this problem.

The right noise background
Some people say they can't study without pop music or a television

in the background. This is seen by some as 'redundancy control' – the need for something to tap their excess mental energy; otherwise it is felt as anxiety. There is no evidence that pop music or any other effect selectively taps any spare mental energy. There is no reason to suppose that *all* mental energy cannot be utilised in the study process anyway. Silence is considered far better than noise for study.

There is an exception, though. It has been found by researchers in this field that some classical music, like that of Bach and Mozart, can actually enhance receptivity. This is because the beat matches the brainwave pattern that a receptive state of mind produces. This is not the case with rock music.

Furthermore, you will not always want to be in a highly receptive suggestible state of mind. You will want to challenge the ideas you are reading. Intelligent scepticism is the state of mind you should aim to achieve. There are no background stimuli known to heighten this.

If silence is the most desirable it is not always possible, whether at home, at school or in the library. If silence is a problem buy yourself some ear-plugs. They are cheap and available from most chemists.

Your physical comfort

What people describe as mental fatigue is, to a large degree, muscular fatigue and much can be done to reduce it. As pointed out in chapter 1, the mind works best when there is least strain upon the body.

Seating

Two parts of the body which will suffer from extended periods of study in a sitting position are the neck and the back. Avoid polyprop chairs. Their shape is designed for cheapness and rigidity, not orthopaedic comfort. Straight backed chairs are best, with a high back if possible.

Your desk

Next you need to check your desk or table height. A reasonable height for most people is 28 to 29 inches from the floor and it is a good idea to have your desk-top tilted towards you. All you need is a piece of chipboard or plyboard propped up a couple of inches at the front. This reduces the need to bend your neck, and so reduces strain, tension and headaches.

One of the best places to position your desk is where your back will be against the window, so that the natural light source shines over your shoulder. However, if you are using a VDU screen there will be a problem with glare, though this can be more or less eliminated with a screen filter.

Air quality and radiation
Glare is not the only problem to contend with if you are using a computer; there is also a current of airborne dust and ELF and VLF radiation, not to mention the electromagnetic field. All of these, some sources say, can affect your health.

For the airborne dust and electromagnetic field an **ioniser** is a worthwhile investment. This is a cheap and effective device which neutralises positive ions in the air arising from the screen's magnetic field. In so doing, it removes the airborne dust particles. You can buy small desk-top ionisers from about £13. You will notice the difference in air quality immediately; it will have the freshness felt in the open air immediately before a thunderstorm.

Screen glare
Screen filters are available which not only reduce almost all the glare but which filter out almost all the ELF and VLF radiation. They range from about £40 to about £120, depending on how well they do their job and whether your screen is flat or curved. The cheaper ones claim to be quite effective, but they are only suitable for flat screens. There is nothing to stop you taping around the edges, though.

Believe it or not another cause of screen glare is spectacles. Light reflects off them onto the screen. Special spectacles for VDU use can be purchased.

It is worth having your eyes tested, anyway. Even a mild astigmatic condition, which is very common, puts more strain on the eyes than need be when you are reading. Such minor faults mean your eyes have to work to correct the image you are seeing. If appropriate spectacles are worn they do not have to do this; eye strain is less and studying does not seem such hard work.

Repetitive strain injury
A problem which has had more publicity is **repetitive strain injury** (RSI) from keyboard usage. This is a real problem. If you are going to do a lot of typing you need to take precautions against it.

1.   Ensure that your keyboard and your seat are the right height.

An ordinary chair will not give you that height without a cushion, though a typist's chair will. The height of a piano stool is what you need to aim for.

2. The keyboard should be placed so that there is room on the desk for your wrists to rest. Having them continuously suspended in the air over the keys is a bad position which can lead to RSI.

ORGANISING YOUR SYSTEM

Having got your space and its conditions organised you now need to attend to the system you are going to operate within it. This will include:

- hardware
- stationery
- books
- storage equipment.

Equipment
The hardware category can be split into essential and non-essential, but useful, items.

Furniture
The essentials include a desk or suitable table. Desks can be purchased second-hand for about £25. Schools and colleges dispose of unwanted desks from time to time. Furniture auctions are another source. If instead you use a table, make sure it is the same height as the desk; otherwise build it up with a sheet of chipboard or blockboard (cheap to buy; most places will cut it to size). Desk tops or table tops should, ideally, be at an angle, sloping towards you, so that you do not have to keep bending your neck down. If you have a desk you would do well to add a sheet of board to the top of it so that such a slope can be achieved.

The next requirement is a suitable chair. Any old chair won't do; you are going to sit studying effectively for extended periods.

Reading lamp
A reading lamp is a cheap essential; they cost only a few pounds. They can ease the strain on your eyes a lot by focussing their light just where you want it. The most useful kind can be clipped onto the back of your chair so that the light falls over your shoulder onto the page.

Stationery

Various items of stationery will be needed; others will be useful but not essential. Obviously notepaper is necessary. Some of the discount stationers and supermarkets now do very cheap bumper packs of A4 lined. Don't throw paper away just because one side has been used, unless you've got money to burn. The other side can be used. Keep a tray of scrap paper within reach.

Correcting fluid, stick adhesive, paperclips, highlighter pens, a stapler and a paper-punch are always useful. With fierce competition between discount stationers things like ring binders can be bought very cheaply. The problem of pages falling out because of torn punch-holes can be avoided by using gummed reinforcer rings. The range of study aids available has grown tremendously in the last few years; the list is too long to deal with here. Visit your local discount stationers to browse.

Non-essential but useful

A home computer is obviously a useful study-aid. Essays look much more professional when typed and they are, of course, easier to read. The computer's 'cut and paste' technique can be used in the production of your work, which is not possible with longhand. Spell-checkers and even grammar-checkers now come as standard with many word-processing software packages.

You are advised not to buy a dedicated word processor, though. Computers can be purchased just as cheaply and they do so much more. A wide range of excellent word-processing software is now available for personal computers. Nor is it a good idea to buy a typewriter in this day and age. A secondhand computer can usually be bought for the same price.

Tape-recorders and personal note-takers can be useful but remember that notes made on them take more time to read than those made on paper, because you can't skim and scan. Furthermore, taking linear notes is less effective than taking diagrammatic notes.

Books

Vocabulary-building

A good dictionary is vital. Don't get a pocket one, get a full sized one. The *Oxford Reference Dictionary* is a good choice.

Roget's Thesaurus is another important element of your tool kit. This is basically a book of similes and associated words. Good English usage requires that we do not repeat words close together in the text. If you want to say the same thing again, find another word which means more or less the same. *Roget's Thesaurus* will give you a whole range of them. All you have to do is look up the word in the index and it will give you the page number where you can find a list of words which mean the same or similar things.

Subject reference

If you are studying at A level or above, a special subject dictionary is an important addition to your bookshelf. Subjects have their own vocabularies of esoteric words (words special to that particular subject) and these are often not found in the *OED (Oxford English Dictionary)*. Penguin publish a range of special subject dictionaries in paperback; they are not expensive.

A further item that you should purchase for your bookshelf is a handbook for each subject you are taking. A handbook is a textbook which covers the entire subject/syllabus and will probably be prescribed by your school or college.

While it is always useful to have to hand as much literature as possible, other texts can be borrowed from the library.

Encyclopaedias are obviously valuable, but they are often prohibitively expensive. Many people will have to rely on their libraries for these, where they will be able to consult them but not take them away.

Literary texts

A word of warning – if your subject is literature, make sure the books you buy are the original texts. There are cheap versions of classics in some shops which are very tempting, but you may find the texts have been altered to make them more comprehensible to a mass readership. Make sure this is not the case before you buy. Penguin paperbacks are an inexpensive option and you can be sure the text is original. Paperbacks are best if you are studying literature; you will not be reluctant to highlight or make notes on the pages as you would with a more expensive hardback.

Articles, pamphlets and magazines can be stored in purpose designed magazine containers on your bookshelf beside your books. Cut down cornflake packets do the job more or less as well.

Filing

You can amass the finest collection of facts and figures in the world, but they are no good if you can't find them when you need them. So often a fact is simply omitted from an essay because the details have been mislaid or the student cannot find the reference place in the book. So plan to set up an efficient filing system.

Indexing

A card-index system is very useful for storing references and notes. A suitable drawer or box can be bought quite cheaply. Whenever a useful snippet of information, a quote or a reference is found, make out a card giving the full bibliographical reference, the page number, the fact or quote and a cross-reference to any other cards with information relating to it.

Note storage

Ring binders are very cheap to buy; they make a tidy and secure way of storing your standard-sized A4 notes. Spacer card sheets can be purchased in sets of different colours and labelled A-Z or 1-30, so that different sections of your notes can be easily identified. One cause of lost notes from ring binders is torn punch-holes. These can be avoided by using gummed reinforcement rings which you can buy at stationers.

If you use a computer, notes and references can be stored on disk, but make sure you keep back-up copies. Store your disks in an appropriate container as they can easily be damaged.

It is best to file documents on a need-to-use basis first and alphabetically second.

- Keep all those files you use at least weekly, arranged in alphabetical order, in the top drawer or a place close to you.

- Keep all those you use less frequently, but at least once a month, in the second drawer.

- Lastly, keep all the rest in the third drawer.

If you are using shelves instead, store the items you use most often in the most easily accessible places. Leave the least accessible places for those you use least. If you are in doubt about what to store where, select everything you have used at least once in the last week for the frequent-use set. Then, out of what's left, take everything that you've needed in the last month as the moderate usage set. Whatever you have left represents the infrequently needed set. As time goes by you can make adjustments.

The benefits of good filing

Not being able to find what you want can be a tempting reason to put things off until later, and all those 'laters' add up. Having the right equipment to hand, the necessary books where you can reach them and an orderly filing system from which you can extract the information you need without difficulty as and when you need it reduces frustration and stress. It also gives you a sense that you are working efficiently, thus increasing confidence and motivation to study.

ORGANISING YOUR TIME

Time slots have different qualities. Different time-scales must be planned for and there is a range of time management aids which can help you.

Qualities of different time slots

Qualities of time slots differ because of physiological, environmental and situational reasons.

Our effectiveness is influenced by a number of natural rhythms, known as *biorhythms*. The circadian rhythm affects us all, but not in the same way. Everyone's energy level is at its lowest very early in the morning and rises gradually towards a peak. While some may peak about midday, others may rise more slowly and not peak until late in the afternoon or early evening.

It is a myth that each hour in the morning is worth much more than each hour in the afternoon. Unquestioning adherence to this principle can result in lower productivity. This, in turn, can lower self-esteem and self concept of ability, causing students who naturally peak later in the day to underestimate their true potential.

Understanding your own natural rhythm

It is important to know your own daily rhythm. This doesn't mean simply how easily you get up in the morning. That has as much – if not more – to do with your evening social habits, which may fit your circadian rhythm no better than your working pattern. You can check your circadian rhythm objectively and reliably using a thermometer.

Make a chart marked with the times of the day, in hours, along the bottom. Mark temperature, in degrees, on the vertical axis. Take your temperature orally an hour after getting up, then at 3-hourly intervals during the day. Take a final reading just before you go to bed. Plot the readings on the chart and join them up.

Repeat the process for a week, carefully plotting the readings on the same chart. Don't expect the lines to match exactly, it is the general shape that is important. At the end of a week you should be able to see clearly where your natural peaks and troughs are, in other words your circadian rhythm. Plan things according to this rather than to a rhythm which someone else tries to tell you is right. It may be right for them, but only this test will tell you if it's right for you.

Some people have more flexible body clocks than others, but to continuously fight against your own natural rhythms is counter-productive.

Female cycles
The female menstrual cycle can have a severe emotional effect on some women. This pre-menstrual tension (PMT) can cause depression. This in turn affects the functioning of the right side of the brain on which spatial skills like mathematics mostly depend. The left side of the brain – used most in language and

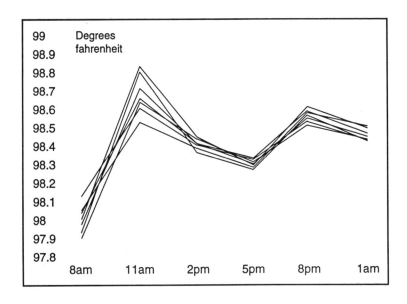

Fig 1. A circadian rhythm chart plotted over 7 days.

sequential processing – is not affected, though.

Women who suffer particularly badly from PMT might try scheduling their linguistic and literary assignments for the part of the month when they suffer most, and keep the unaffected times for any mathematics, science or fine art work. Similarly, they could consider doing the research for all their assignments during the unaffected weeks and leave the writing-up for the difficult days.

Environmental cycles
Our bodies are also influenced by cycles in our environment. Light, and so length of day, determines the secretion of the sleep-inducing hormone melatonin. For some people the effect is so severe that it causes a cyclical kind of depression (Seasonal Affective Disorder or SAD) in the winter months.

Different phases of the day
The suitability of study environment will vary throughout the day. For some students there will be more peace and quiet in the mid-morning or afternoon. Family members or flatmates may be constantly around in the early morning and in the evenings, rushing to get ready for school or work in the mornings – playing music or watching television in the evenings. This has to be taken into account in your plan. You need to plot time-slots when you can rely on uninterrupted peace.

University libraries are often quietest and least crowded in the evenings. City libraries are often least quiet between 4.15pm and 5.00pm when school children use them to do homework while waiting for their parents to collect them.

There are also times of the day when certain aspects of study are simply not possible. Library research, for example, cannot be done after 10pm at most universities. College libraries tend to close around 9pm and town libraries often close at 5.00pm.

The pre-exam period
Nearing the exams the quality of your time will change for psycho-physiological reasons. The increasing stress level will make your thinking more difficult, and make it harder to grapple with new ideas. The closer you get to the exam date the more your efforts should be devoted to simple memorising, regurgitation of facts and practice in using principles which you have already learned. Some recurring situations lend themselves well to some aspects of study. Waiting periods are one of them. Advertisers have long

realised the receptive state of people's minds when they are waiting for a bus; that's why you see advertisements for the really high-profile products on bus shelters. These sites are expensive, because they are so effective. When people are waiting they are bored and they want something to think about. If you wait for buses regularly, or wait in your car, or a reception area, for a friend, partner or child, use this period constructively. Use it to go over notes, read up on a subject, or think through ideas you have noted from lectures.

Different time-scales

Your course will be split up into sections and each one has its own intermediate objectives which, taken together, will fulfil the overall objective of attainment of proficiency and the qualification you set out to achieve. You should plan your study with these different timescales in mind. They include

- course
- year
- term
- week
- day
- essay/project

Much of your course-long and year-long timescales will be dictated by your course syllabus, although those who are studying independently or doing research degrees will have to make their own plans.

Term planning
Term planning will involve plotting your

1. continuous assessment requirements
2. class and lecture attendance
3. personal-social arrangements.

It will involve allocating time for each assignment and taking account of the natural cycle effects mentioned earlier.

The week-long timescale is plotted on a timetable. It will feature the allocation of daily time-slots. Day-long planning involves appreciation of the different time-slot qualities mentioned earlier and appropriate allocation of time on that basis. Such planning will then be included in your weekly timetable.

Essay and project planning
Essay/project-long planning amounts to splitting up the job in question into different tasks:

- researching
- writing the first draft
- editing
- writing the final 'fair copy' to hand in.

Each task is taxing in a different way and different phases of the day are suitable. For researching you need peace and quiet, maximum mental alertness and open libraries; daytime is likely to be best, close to your natural energy peak.

Writing the first draft needs alertness too, but the library doesn't have to be open. It requires quiet, so, for some, evenings might not be appropriate.

Editing is not so taxing and can be done when time-quality is not so good, though it depends on the degree of editing involved.

Spell-checking can be done even when it's noisy, or when you are a little tired, but critical evaluation of ideas requires some keenness of mind.

Writing or typing up the final copy requires neither peak alertness, open libraries nor absolutely quiet, uninterrupted spans of time. It can be done when more challenging tasks could not, saving the best times for those jobs.

An adult is expected to be able to write around 1,000 words an hour, writing continuously. Many people can write much more and many much less, but this is an average figure on which further and higher education exams are based. For a 2,000 word essay, therefore, allow about two hours for writing up each of the first and final copies. A reasonable time to allow for research is two to four hours for such an essay; editing of the first draft can be expected to take about an hour. That gives you a guide to start with. You may need to adjust it to suit your own abilities in each stage of essay writing.

Final revision timetable
As you approach the exams you need to work out a revision timetable. Split your subjects up into chunks and then allocate equal time to each. Don't be tempted to say, 'I need more time on

this because I am not so sure of the principles yet'.

If you don't know them by then you can't reasonably expect to know them by the exam. When the exam is only days away your stress level will be relatively high. This will reduce your ability to grapple with new ideas. If you couldn't grasp them when stress was not high you are much less likely to do so now. Keep this period for rehearsing what you have grasped.

Time management aids

There are a number of products which can be purchased quite cheaply to help you organise your time.

For year-long planning, 'academic year-planner wall-charts' are available at discount stationers for less than the price of a 'Big Mac'. Sometimes banks and building societies give them away free to students as part of a sales promotion. These are very useful; a year-long picture of your course requirements and your plan for fulfilling them, helps you keep things in the right perspective.

You can't carry your year planner around with you, nor can you enter the kind of detail you need for day to day planning. A diary is the thing for planning on this time-scale.

For week by week planning of regular commitments, make out a single-sheet timetable. On this you can even colour the different time qualities of the day.

For a few pounds you can buy a looseleaf personal organiser, in which there are pre-printed forms for many of the time-planning functions – diary, year planner, project planner and more.

SCHEDULING WORK, REST AND PLAY

It is easy to expect too much of yourself, to think you are going to work all hours and have no time off for a month, but it is unlikely to work out in practice. Human nature is not like that. It is important for you to schedule time off for rest, exercise and play.

Optimum study periods

For most people the optimum length period for serious library research on a mentally taxing subject is about two hours, with strictly planned and controlled breaks of five minutes on the hour. The more you get into your subject the longer you'll be able to, and want to, study for. Your study sessions can slowly lengthen as you master the material. In the early stages of your course, frequent shorter periods are appropriate; but as you approach proficiency much longer periods of study are called for because of the complexity of material you have to grapple with and the greater motivation which comes with the awareness of your developing mastery.

In chapter 1 it was pointed out that continued mental work causes physical fatigue. The body needs rest from the postural strains that prolonged periods of 'head down' study puts upon it – not to mention the eye strain and repetitive wrist and lower arm strain if you are using a typewriter or computer.

Furthermore, while the brain doesn't, itself, get tired, long periods of grappling with difficult ideas will cause an emotional drain. Stress and self-esteem damage can arise when mastery is proving difficult, or failure experienced. You will feel boredom at times, too, when your reading matter seems uninteresting or repetitive. The emotional recharging function of the smile is important to our feeling of well-being, but it is unlikely to happen during long periods of concentration. So you will progressively feel tired and your effectiveness will wane if you don't budget for regular periods of rest and relaxation.

Using rest periods

Don't just sit around in your rest periods; schedule them to include periods of

- exercise
- relaxation
- fun.

If you don't map out your free-period activities after a long period of intense study you will simply not be able to switch off. Lie on the settee by the television and after half an hour you will realise you haven't been following the film; your mind is still on your work.

Exercise will relieve the stiffness in the joints and muscles caused by the lack of physical action during study. It will also help to retain your physical health, for we are made for physical action, but we don't get much of it during academic work. Planned social recreation will give you plenty of opportunity to smile, and so recharge your emotional batteries.

DEALING WITH SETBACKS

Even the best laid plans can go wrong. Your plans may have been undermined because you have:

- been ill
- mismanaged your time
- forgotten you had an essay to do
- underestimated the work needed for an assignment
- overspent on time for another project and left insufficient for this one
- lost your notes
- lost your completed assignment.

You will not get a good mark for a rushed assignment, put together in a hurry because of lack of time, or because an earlier attempt was lost. But that does not mean you should just give up. If a car ran over your foot you wouldn't say, 'Now here's my head, you might as well run over that too.' So don't think in this negative way if you suffer a setback to your coursework. Just because you may not get a good mark it is no reason to admit defeat and get no mark at all.

Emergency tactics
What can you do as an emergency measure?

Lost notes
Borrow someone else's and copy them, then re-organize them to suit your way of thinking.

Missed lectures
1. Borrow notes from a friend.

2. Consider private tuition, though this is not really relevant for university courses, as they are very institution-specific, so there will not be the supply of private tutors who know the syllabuses.

No time to finish an essay
1. Structure the skeleton of the essay, labelling the type of material you might have used if you had it (ie do an essay plan).

2. Fill in what you can from a commonsense approach. Mention any relevant authors or other authority figures which you know of and any relevant books as and where appropriate.

3. Get hold of whatever books you can on the subject and use the

following drastically rapid technique for extracting their essence:

    (a) Read the contents list.
        Read the introduction.
        Read the summary.

    (b) Try to formulate an idea of what the book is about from this alone.

    (c) If you have time to read up more than just introductions and summaries you will still have to be very selective. Seek out principles, scanning and skimming the text to do so. Look for terms like 'The point is...' and 'What I am saying is...' What follows, in a nutshell, is what the author has been talking about for perhaps many paragraphs and perhaps even whole chapters. You can save yourself a lot of time if you learn to do this.

4. Ask for an extension, but be careful not to jeopardise subsequent study plans.

A final word

Environment has a big effect on achievement and you can do much to control it. You can't work without adequate tools. They don't have to be expensive or high-tech, but choosing wisely will pay dividends. There is much more to time management than seems obvious at first glance and careful attention to this and the other factors mentioned can really give you the edge in the success stakes.

SUMMARY

1. Be realistic in your planning.
2. Study in an undisturbed environment.
3. Organise your working area to minimise physical fatigue and maximise effective study.
4. Buy a good dictionary, thesaurus, manual on good English usage and special subject dictionaries for the courses you are taking.
5. Organise your filing system. File on a frequency of use basis.
6. Exploit the fact that time quality varies throughout each day.
7. Plan in different timescales.
8. Plan for work, rest and play.

CASE STUDIES

Tom hates to plan

Tom Eliot does not plan much. 'Blow all that year-planner stuff. I can't even keep my floor tidy, so there's little point in starting on my mind,' he says.

He leaves essays until the last minute and then there is a mad dash to meet the deadline. At such times he 'burns the midnight oil'. Propped up on one elbow, he scribbles away on an A4 pad on his bed, with three textbooks spread out on the pillow. The spelling is never perfect; Tom only has a pocket dictionary, and he finds it such a pain to keep looking up words he's not sure of. Tom usually achieves average or slightly below average marks.

Jennifer's strategy

Jennifer Goss expects a lot of herself, but she's realistic, too. She knows that if she puts herself under relentless pressure every hour of every day she simply won't keep to it. She builds leisure activities into her grand plan for achievement.

Her study periods are intensive – no sitting in the kitchen with her books while the others in the house chatter away. She shuts herself in her room, where she has everything organized for maximum productivity.

Karen overdoes it

Karen Morris plans rigorously, because she has been told to. She is not realistic about it, though. She doesn't allow herself much leisure time in her plans. Consequently, they often go wrong.

Karen tends to sit and study in an armchair, but all she does is sit and read from a textbook over and over again.

She files all her neatly written notes, in strict order, in a ring binder, even though they are little more than verbatim transcripts of the lectures.

DISCUSSION POINTS

1. List five things you could do to make your working environment better.

2. How does your time quality vary throughout the day?

3. How much rest and play do you include in your planning? Have you got the balance right? If not, how might you change it?

3
Finding the Information

ASSESSING YOUR STUDY SKILLS

How good are your study skills? Start by rating yourself as honestly as you can.

Self assessment of study skills

Study skill	Above Average	Average	Below Average
Reading speed	☐	☐	☐
Reading comprehension	☐	☐	☐
Vocabulary	☐	☐	☐
Preparation for classes and lectures	☐	☐	☐
Participation in class discussion	☐	☐	☐
Note-taking skills	☐	☐	☐
Library-using skills	☐	☐	☐
Essay-writing skills	☐	☐	☐

Some students think they can rely on cramming, but it is not really effective. Cramming is known to be subject to rapid forgetting, so the further away from exam dates it is done, the more futile the effort will be. To achieve highly you need well developed study skills.

HANDLING CLASSES

Attendance

The 'teacher expectations' effect is a known influence on achievement. Teachers will naturally expect more from pupils who attend classes regularly and punctually than from those who do not. Otherwise, they would believe that their teaching had little effect on their pupils' progress.

Similarly, teachers will see students who submit coursework punctually as making better progress than those who do not. It is foolhardy for students to think they can escape with such a casual approach to their course.

Many students simply turn up to classes not knowing what to expect. Their heads are like clean slates waiting to be written upon. This is a very passive approach. It is characteristic of those destined for a very mediocre grade at the end of their course. To achieve highly you must get involved.

Preparation

It is important to prepare for classes in advance. Sometimes your tutor will prescribe some form of preparatory work. Very often this is a set piece of reading. If he does not it is no reason to assume that no reading should be done. From the course syllabus, the course handbook and any prescribed supplementary reading, you will be able to tell in advance topics which will be discussed. If you know anyone who took the same course last year you will be able to predict with even greater certainty. Prepare a list of questions and arguments. Work out your opinions on the subject and be ready to voice them.

Participating

Just as teachers will expect better results from students who attend regularly, so they will from students who participate most in class. If you participate you'll understand more, and enjoy it more. Active involvement also slows down the rate of forgetting.

Work out in advance what is going to be brought up in class, then you will be ready to deal with it in a useful way. After all, this is how we handle everyday life. If we didn't guess ahead of events we would approach every new situation – every conversation, story, experience – completely unprepared. We would handle them very poorly indeed. Although you may not be aware of it, even when you are listening to a friend telling you something you are guessing ahead what he is going to tell you. Members on the floor of the House of Commons would be in a fine mess if they didn't make careful guesses about what issues and questions their opponents would raise. The next time you see a television news report from the House of Commons, watch how questions from the Opposition are met with carefully constructed responses. These are the product of a guessing game.

Teachers aim to deal with up to half a dozen major points in a lesson. How do you spot what they are? They are likely to be the main points in the section of the course handbook relating to the lesson in question. This is why it's important to refer to the textbook before the lesson. You can home in more closely on how the teacher intends to handle the material by comparing the textbook with the course essay questions, if they are given out in advance, and with questions from past exam papers, which will be available in the library. Study of past exam papers is a very useful means of focusing your studies. It is ignored by a surprising number of students.

• Offer your opinions in class discussion.

• If you don't understand anything, say so.

• If you don't know what else to say, ask what the practical applications of the knowledge being discussed are. Make suggestions about these.

Even if you are bored with the lesson, on no account show it. Teachers are unlikely to see it as due to their performance or to the subject; to them, it is probably fascinating. They are more likely to interpret your boredom as your unsuitability for the course and so expect only mediocre achievement – and teacher prophecies have a self-fulfilling nature.

It is best to make your debut as a class speaker early in the year, while most of your fellow students are still too shy. There will be less competition for the airwaves and you'll probably get less opposition; this will boost your self-confidence ready for the days when the others feel secure enough to challenge what is said.

If you want to give your tutor high expectations of your progress show him/her that you have such expectations yourself. Ask if you can discuss your progress from time to time.

HANDLING LECTURES

For some people, lectures are rather like photocopiers. Information is copied from one person's notepad (the lecturer's) to another's (the student's) without passing through the student's head on the way. This is a sad misuse of a valuable learning resource.

The functions of lectures are as follows:

- to present material not available elsewhere
- to explain the more obscure points
- to direct further reading.

Listening and concentrating

Sit where you can see and hear. Do not sit at the back, if you can help it, nor by a door or window where you may be distracted. Sit up in an alert posture; do not slouch. If your posture is alert, your mind will follow suit. This concordance of mind and body has been well tested by psychologists.

It is not the lecturer, but what he is saying, that is important. Don't be distracted by the lecturer's appearance or manners. Don't let your attention stray to surveying the other students in the seats of the lecture hall, and don't doodle. Attend intelligently. You can join an audience to be entertained in the theatre or cinema any day of the week, but your lecture on this subject will come round only once; miss it, and you will lose out.

Note-taking at lectures

How much note-taking should you do? Some students take no notes at all. They remember virtually nothing, either. Others write down practically every word, sometimes even asking the lecturer to stop to verify whether the last word was 'that' or 'which'. These people get little out of lectures either.

As mentioned earlier, comprehending involves guessing ahead. You can't do this while you're writing in 'real-time' mode.

The answer is: note key words and phrases only, and helpful examples given by the lecturer. Nor do you even need to write these in full. Instead, use short forms, eg 'stats' (statistics), # (psychology), and other abbreviations.

Develop your own personal shorthand. Adult students may have learned conventional shorthand or speedwriting, eg Pitmans, especially if they have worked in offices or journalism. This will be a great advantage to them, but it may not be a wise use of time for other students to learn them merely for studying another subject. Personalised shorthand codes are quite adequate.

Some people take tape recorders into lectures. This is not an advisable practice for two reasons:

1. It may lead you to be more casual about whether you really grasp what the lecturer is saying, knowing you can listen to it later. You will not be exercising your listening skills, and so those skills will not improve.

2. This form of record is even more restrictive than linear notes. On tape you cannot skim through as you can on paper. Remember, the aim is to 'extract the wheat from the chaff'. You don't do that by examining every grain, which is, indeed, what you are doing when you 'chug – chug – chug' through the material on tape. It is a very inefficient method of note-taking.

Taking an active approach

Just as in classwork, you'll get more out of lectures if you take an active approach. That doesn't mean you can discuss things, as you can in class, but you can mentally interact with what the lecturer is saying. Such an approach enhances comprehension and motivation and also reduces forgetting.

First of all, assess what the main points of the lecture are. Lecturers generally aim to deal with only between a couple and half a dozen points in a lecture.

You may find that particular points have not been explained very well. If so, grapple with them using your own knowledge and experience. You may need to make a brief note to remind you to think about them, or discuss them with other students and/or your tutor later on.

HANDLING GROUP WORK

In seminars tutors may ask selected students to give a talk on a chosen part of the subject to the rest of the group. Students may be asked – or may themselves ask for reasons of shyness – to share the task with others. This will require teamwork in the gathering of information and in how it is to be presented.

Group dynamics

Students suddenly become aware of 'group dynamics' in these situations. You will see how people fall into particular roles, one perhaps taking the lead and having most to say, another keeping things together and maintaining a sense of proportion.

One member may assume the role of writing down the plan. The whole group may rely on an extrovert member to keep the enthusiasm going, while a more introverted character, like the wise old owl sitting on the oak, will say little, but hear much and think even more. Consequently, when he does speak it will be to point out something the others would not have thought of because of their more superficial treatment of the subject. The presentation may then be made by a volunteer or this task may be shared by more than one person.

Some groups integrate well, and those which do may have a joint brainstorming session followed by highly collaborative work in collecting the information.

Not all groups integrate so well, though. Some experience conflict: after all, the group may consist of people who would not normally seek each other's company. In this case, it may be best for the group to split the topic up into sub-topics, leaving each party to concentrate on a different part. This way they are all in charge of their own thing, but still working as a team.

Tutor direction of the group

At other times tutorials will involve group discussions. Tutors vary tremendously in the freedom they permit in such sessions. I have witnessed a range of tutor-directiveness from more or less total uninvolvement, which can leave students bewildered about why they are there, to more or less total control by the tutor, so that the only real difference between that and a lecture is that the teacher is sitting down.

In the middle ground tutorials often involve the tutor introducing a topic and throwing out a question every now and then when the discussion dries up. Often they will shepherd the discussion from one topic to another so that the planned range of ideas is dealt with.

The benefits of group study

The purpose of tutorials is to give students a chance to test on their classmates the ideas and skills they have learned from lectures and reading. This way they can assess whether their view of things is reasonable.

It doesn't necessarily mean you are wrong if the others disagree with you. It may mean you need to reconsider; it may merely show that they have different values from yours. People's basic assumptions about what is right or wrong, or good or bad, influence the weight they give to different things. You are unlikely to convince an ardent socialist that privatisation of the railways is economically advantageous, nor an ardent capitalist that it's not.

Group discussions allow students to share information they have discovered and to clarify ideas they have not understood.

Preparing yourself for group work

Group work is scheduled because of the particular benefits it provides to students. Consequently, you have a duty both to yourself and to the other students, to become involved. It is important, therefore, to prepare for such discussions, just as you would for classwork and lectures.

The job of guessing which points will be raised is rather more challenging here. What is important, and easier, is to anticipate the challenges you will receive to the points you intend to make. You can never really say you know your subject well, until you have considered all the known lines of argument. It is important, therefore, to prepare your responses to those challenges in advance. Surprise challenges, which you have not allowed for, are a bonus. If you have a sincere will to learn, these challenges will give the tutorial discussion a rewarding feel for you.

Be prepared to speak up and contribute to the discussion. Be assertive, but not aggressive. Being assertive is insisting on your right to your own opinion, but accept that other people have the right to theirs. Being aggressive is a bullying insistence that you are right and everyone else is wrong; do this and you will soon find yourself crowded out when you try to speak, or simply ignored. Remember, it is a 'group' discussion: don't hog it. It is the richness and range of contributions that is important. But do contribute; don't sit on the sidelines and let others do the work. If there are twelve people in a one-hour tutorial group it is unreasonable for you to expect to take up ten minutes of the total airtime, though nobody is going to be exactly counting unless you really overdo it.

USING LIBRARIES

One of the main resources for college study is the library. It is important that you know your way around the system.

To go into a library and simply browse along the shelves for sources of information is like reading a textbook from cover to cover. It is wasteful in terms of time and it is academically very unproficient.

At the start of each academic year a **library tutorial** may be offered to new students of a particular course, and to anyone at the college or university who wishes to attend. Look out for it and don't miss the opportunity.

The library staff will also always be willing to help you. In university libraries specialist librarians will be able to point you towards particular sources for your subject.

Reading lists

You will be given reading lists by your lecturers. Go straight to where those books or articles are stored. There will invariably be a bank of computers, together with a menu-driven set of instructions, which are very easy to follow. From this you will be able quickly to tell the exact shelf position of the book you are seeking, if indeed it is held by the library and is not currently out on loan. If the library doesn't keep it, you will be able to order it at the **inter-library loans** desk. If the item is out on loan (which you can also ascertain from the computer) you will be able to reserve it at the desk for when it is returned by the present borrower. There will probably be a tray of reserve slips on the desk for this purpose.

Assuming the book is currently on the shelves, there will be a plan on the wall showing the position in the library where the shelf-reference can be found.

You may want to browse through titles on a particular subject area. To do this you can key in – using the appropriate command on the computer's menu – the subject code and scroll through the titles available.

It is always best to concentrate on the most recent sources, but sometimes older works will be required. Sometimes you will find these are not included on the computer; their shelf references must be found by looking through the card-indices. There are usually two sets of these – one arranged by author order, the other by subject.

Many town libraries do not yet have their records on computer. Often their records will be in the form of microfiches, which are filed in 'author' and 'subject' order, in a special holder placed next to a microfiche reader unit for use by the public.

Using the Dewey Decimal System

Many libraries classify their books using the Dewey Decimal System. This is simply a system whereby the books are classified according to ten classifications:

000	General	500	Pure sciences
100	Philosophy	600	Useful arts
200	Religion	700	Fine arts
300	Social sciences	800	Literature
400	Philology	900	History

These classes are each subdivided into ten sub-classes, and each of those a further ten.

Some libraries, however, use a system of letters and numbers, but the classification strategy is similar.

You may want to look up the books on a particular area, or by a particular author, which you know are currently in print, but not presently held by the library of your university or college. The source for this is *The British National Bibliography*, in the reference section (where all the encyclopaedias and dictionaries are). The *BNB* is a highly up-to-date source of information on books, published weekly, annually and five-yearly.

There are also many specialist bibliographies containing information about books on specific subjects.

Another major reference book you may sometimes need is the *Oxford English Dictionary*, which has ten volumes and supplements.

Using abstracts

Abstracts are digests of articles on a particular subject. Periodically (eg annually) the articles in leading specialist journals are summarised and bound, so that you can browse through and quickly decide which articles would be of value to you. The full bibliographical references are included, so that you can look up the complete article in the journal concerned.

The last year or so's supply of such journals will be available in the periodicals section of the library. All copies from previous years will have been bound in volumes covering periods of, for example, a year or half-year, and placed on the library shelves. More will be said about the important role of periodicals later in this chapter.

There are also indices of periodicals available.

'Out of print' books, periodicals and newspapers are often available on microfilm. If you need them ask at the desk.

Following the clues

Because of the ever-changing nature of knowledge, the most recent works are always preferable.

The most up-to-date works are likely to be found as articles in periodicals. It takes less time to get an article into print than it does a book. Researchers will eventually publish their full knowledge in a book, but they invariably publish their interim findings in journals.

Begin in the periodicals section of the library. Look at the indices of all the periodicals which would be likely to have information relevant to the assignment you are doing. There may be a few months supply of each, as it may be only once a year that they are bound in volumes. The titles of the indices should suggest the content of the journals concerned.

If you find any relevant articles, read and take notes. Also, copy the bibliographies to the articles. Look up the books and periodical articles in them which seem relevant to your task. When you find information from those that is useful to you note it down and copy the bibliographies to these articles too. Repeat this process for as long as you are finding valuable information, or for as long as your time-scale permits.

When you have exhausted this route, go to the abstracts, for you need to consult the periodicals of previous years, which have been bound and shelved elsewhere. Abstracts are classified compilations of articles which have appeared in major journals. Look for recent articles relevant to your assignment, and repeat the above process. Carry on until you have enough information. Remember, you will never be able to include it all. You will have neither the time, nor the word space. This way at least you will have concentrated on the most up-to-date information.

What can you do if your reading list prescribes a book which the library holds only one copy of and you can't find an alternative? Ask the librarian for guidance on sources of information on that topic. In university libraries there will be a specialist librarian for each area and he or she should have a good idea where to start. Never be afraid to ask if you can't find something in the library.

DEVELOPING YOUR READING SKILLS

Reading for pleasure and reading to learn

Reading to learn is different to reading for pleasure. In the latter you relax and let the material work on you. Reading to learn it's the other way round. You must be in the driving seat and decide what *you* want from the text.

To start with, check your reading speed. Take a page of a story you have not read, from some source with a middle-of-the-road level of difficulty; the *Reader's Digest* is a reasonable choice for the purpose. Time yourself reading it. Make sure the page is 100% text – no pictures or diagrams. Count the number of words on the page and divide it by the number of minutes it took you to read it. This will give you a reading speed in words per minute. Repeat the process for two more pages and average out the three reading speeds you have measured (add the three together and divide by three). If your reading speed is below 275 wpm it is very slow. Serious attention needs to be given to improving it.

There are two main reasons for slow reading

- slow movement along the lines

- narrow wordspan (the number of words viewed at a glance)

Software for improving your reading speed is available for home computers.

As you develop your reading skill you should test it frequently to make sure you are not slipping back. Be sure that you always understand the material.

Many slow readers argue that they read slowly because they do not want to miss anything. However, studies show that slow reading results in less information intake than fast reading.

Psychological studies have shown that the speed with which we process information in our heads determines the difficulty we experience with the ideas. Information we take in doesn't stay very long before it decays. If we do not quickly connect all the bits of an idea together, before some of them disappear, we won't grasp the idea. This is what we describe as 'difficulty in understanding something'.

Only when you've managed to link the individual bits together into a meaningful idea will your mind accept it as something to store for good, so the less you understand the less you'll remember.

Other things which slow people down are 'pointing with the finger' and silently speaking the words. If you have these habits get out of them.

Nor should you focus your eyes on each word at a time. The human eyes can scan several words at a time, and certainly at least three without difficulty. Moreover, it's not the words that give you the information. If you think about it, it's the spaces between. The spaces between represent the connection between two words and it's this connection which makes up the complete idea. If you only look at the words, therefore, you will 'not see the wood for the trees'.

Here is a reason for developing as wide a word-span as you can. Understanding occurs where the eyes fix on a section of the line, not when they are moving along it to the next section. The wider your word-span the less fixations per line and the less time spent moving in between fixations. Consequently, more of the time is spent in 'understanding mode'. You should certainly not let yourself go on making more than three or four eye fixations per line in an A5 size textbook.

Another way to improve your intake of reading matter is to train yourself to think in terms of reading 'thought units' rather than words.

Reading skill is type-specific; you can be good with fiction, but not with non-fiction and vice versa. Fiction reading skill is different to non-fiction technique. Even then the technique will depend on whether you are reading for pleasure or reading to critically appraise. If you are reading for pleasure you will read more passively, allowing the language to have its effect upon you. If you are reading to appraise critically you will be looking out for particular things, trying to detect the author's point of view, such as irony, or how the author has used imagery to reinforce theme, or how he has made the characters plausible.

Improving your reading skill

To improve you have to establish what your present level of skill is, set yourself a programme for improvement and stick to it. Test yourself regularly, at least every six months.

There is much 'redundancy' in written language. In speech we can continuously check whether the listener understands by asking for a grunt or a nod, or by noticing whether they are hanging onto the argument or looking totally confused. In written language this is not possible. Writers therefore tend to say the same thing in more than one way to increase the chances of the right message getting through. If you can get straight to the message and understand it without having to read the excess wording (the redundancy) you can save yourself a lot of time.

Another thing which handicaps reading speed is 'compulsive regression' – the tendency to keep looking back. If you have this habit, get out of it.

Limited vocabulary can also be a problem. If you are in doubt about the meaning of words you will tend to go back over the sentence to try to guess it. More will be said about improving your vocabulary later.

Using the questioning technique

Raise some questions before you begin reading a text. This will make your mind work in a critical manner, making your reading active rather than passive. Tests have shown that this improves reading speed by around 24%.

How do you know what question to ask? One of the best ways is to use the writer's headings, turning statements into questions. Writers choose headings carefully, to reflect the main focus of the material which follows.

Headings tend to be of different types, reflecting their different levels of importance. Those which are centred tend to be more important than those which are not. Sometimes headings are numbered and this can help you get an idea of how many major points the author wants you to pick up.

Sometimes authors themselves pose questions in the text. You can, if you wish, include these in your questions, or use them as a guide to formulate your own.

Another way of formulating questions is to base them on any supplementary material you have been asked to read, for example asking how far that material is dealt with in this text, or how far the material you are about to read relates to it.

It also helps to raise questions after you have read a section. This has two functions:

- It confirms the accuracy of your reading.

- It slows down the rate of forgetting.

Ask yourself such things as:

- Do I understand it?

- Does it make sense?

- Is it relevant?

- Do I agree with it?

- Is it challengeable?

- How does it relate to the other course material?

- How does it fit in with the course objectives?

- Does it help me do this, or any of the other essays?

Looking for signposts

As you read the text look out for 'signpost' words and phrases. Authors often place clear clues to understanding their material. Examples are in such phrases as 'What I am saying is...'. What follows a phrase like this is likely to be what the author has, perhaps spent several paragraphs communicating. If you understand this you can save yourself a lot of time. Other examples are:

> 'To put it another way...'
> 'In other words...'

Each of these are meant to amplify the point the author is making. Sometimes such phrases will be used to indicate what the author is emphasizing. Examples are:

> 'Most importantly...'
> 'Most of all...'
> 'Above all...'
> 'Especially...'

Some signposts give clues to the ordering of the ideas the author is communicating, for example:

> 'When...'
> 'After...'
> 'Afterwards...'
> 'Before...'

An agenda of key points

Sometimes authors use numbers to tell the readers how many points they need to grasp, for example:

> 'There are four things to be aware of...'
> 'The two main points to note are...'

Look also for numbered sentences, they serve the same purpose, for example:

> 1)..., 2..., 3)...

Sometimes letters are used instead of numbers, for example:

> a)..., b)..., c)...

Sometimes numbers written in words are used for the same purpose, eg.

> 'Firstly...'
> 'Secondly...'
> 'Thirdly...'

Changing direction
When the author is 'changing tack' he is likely to give the reader clues with words or phrases, such as:

> 'On the other hand...'
> 'However...'
> 'Nevertheless...'
> 'In contrast...'
> 'Conversely...'

Explaining causes and effects
When the author is explaining the cause or effect of anything he may use terms like

> 'Because...'
> 'Consequently...'
> 'Since...'
> 'The reason is...'
> 'With the effect that...'
> 'Accordingly...'
> 'Thus...'
> 'Hence...'
> 'Then...'
> 'Therefore...'

Topic and summary sentences
Look out for topic sentences. These are sentences at the start of a paragraph which tell you what the whole paragraph is about. For more information on these see page 85.

Look also for summary sentences, as these contain the main ideas in concise form. Sometimes these will begin with phrases like:

> 'To summarise...'
> 'In summary...'

Handling non-verbal material

Pay particular attention to all non-verbal material, for example:

- tables
- graphs
- charts
- diagrams
- maps.

Authors use these to back up, or clarify, the most important points.

Learning from graphs

You can extract the most important message from a graph quickly by looking at the title, the legend (a label which explains what the units on both axes mean) and the trend line, *eg* whether it is rising or falling. If the line is straight, it suggests a clear and direct relationship between the two variables. If not, it may still be easy to spot a generally rising or falling trend. If the line curves upwards there may be an **exponential** relationship, where one variable has an increasing effect on the other. More will be said about this in chapter 5.

You have to be careful when interpreting graphs and charts. They can be constructed in such a way that they give a false impression. A trend line showing continuously rising profits over nine months may conceal the fact that there was an enormous loss in the three month period before the graph starts.

Pictograms

Pictograms are particularly deceptive. These are basically bar charts with pictures instead of bars. To keep the pictures in proportion each increase vertically is matched by an increase horizontally. Consequently, increases appear greater than they actually are. Consider the example in figure 2.

Study all scientific diagrams carefully. The author is unlikely to include details which are not important to the point being made.

Marking textbooks

Some students are reluctant to mark or highlight their textbooks. But why not? What have you bought them for if not to learn? If marking them aids learning (and we know it does) then it makes sense.

Don't overdo it, though, as many do. Otherwise you will end up

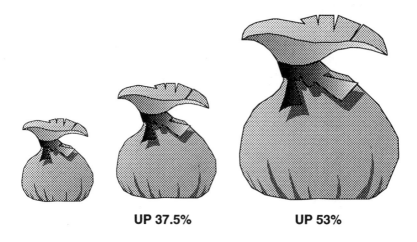

UP 37.5%   **UP 53%**

Fig. 2. Return on XYZ Unit Trust over a 3-month period
from May 1st to August 1st.

with so many marks that you will lose sight of what is most important. One of the things which leads to over-marking is marking as you read. Don't mark until you've read a whole section. Only then will you be able to see what the important points were.

But how much is a whole section of text? About twenty lines (say half-a-page) is appropriate for the average student. Formulate questions for each section of about this length.
What should you mark?

- Underline, or highlight, **key words and phrases**.
- Circle any specifically important **terms** used.
- Connect **related points** to each other with a line.
- Summarise, in the margin, the **ideas** which each heading refers to.

These markings make things clearer, and complete the relationship between what the author is trying to tell you, and how you understand it.

Handling words
A poor vocabulary will limit both your reading speed and understanding. Try to improve your vocabulary if you really want to do well.

Common roots of words

The linguist J. Brown reported that about 60% of words in common use in English have Greek or Latin roots. Consequently, you can often work out the meaning of one word from your knowledge of others. If you've a smattering of Latin knowledge you have an advantage. The roots from which English words derive are given in any good dictionary. Attention to these will help you grapple better with new words.

Word prefixes and suffixes

Many English words have prefixes, like 'mis', 'un', or 'dis', for example. These prefixes have common meanings 'wrongly', 'not' and 'the reverse of', respectively.

Similarly, English words have suffixes, like 'ism', and 'graphy' meaning 'the principles of', in the case of 'ism' and 'the descriptive science of', or 'manner of writing' in the case of 'graphy'.

Using a dictionary

It is important that you obtain a good dictionary. The *Oxford Reference Dictionary* is a good choice for home use. A problem in using a dictionary, especially if you enjoy words, is that the book itself is interesting. Some students open the dictionary to look up one word and become fascinated by other words they see close by. Suddenly it's 5.30pm and the library is closing. Words are interesting, but avoid this temptation; it will destroy your time-plan.

Specialist vocabulary

Different sub-disciplines such as psychology, sociology, economics, physics and biology have their own special 'esoteric' words. You may not find these in a standard dictionary, so you should invest in a specialist dictionary for your subject. These are usually available in paperback and are not expensive. In addition, particular sub-disciplines use general words in special ways. For example, the word 'work' means a totally different thing to a physicist to that which it means to a sociologist. Each time you meet a new word, reinforce your knowledge of it. One way is to use that word at least three times that day. Another is to make vocabulary cards and file them near at hand to run through them and so reinforce your memory. Write the word on the front of the card; on the back write the dictionary definition, plus a sentence containing the word. Make a mark on the top right hand corner every time you fail to recall what the word means. This is the kind of thing you can do at 'waiting times', or other short intervals if you keep a few such cards in your pocket.

The SQ3R method

F. P. Robinson developed a formula for efficient reading which he called SQ3R. It stands for:

Skim
Question
Read
Recite
Review

Skim

First you glance through a section of a chapter to get a rough idea what it is about. If there is a summary, read that too. Look out for between three and six ideas. Allow yourself no more than one minute for this part of the process.

Question

Next you should make a question from the first heading.

Read

Then you read that section through with the aim of answering that question.

Recite

Afterwards, turn away from the book and try to summarise what you have read. Jot your summary down on paper. If you are unable to do so, glance quickly through it again.

Review

When you have done this for each section in the chapter write a brief outline of how the main points of each section relate to each other; make sure that you include the sub-points to the main points in your summary.

This is a proven method which has been found to lead to a 66% improvement in reading speed and 25% in accuracy.

The OK4R method

A more advanced formula, which grew from this, is the OK4R

method. It stands for:

Overview
Key ideas
Read
Recall
Reflect
Review

Overview

First you seek to get an overview of the book using the contents list, the introduction and the summary. Read any topic sentences at the beginning of chapters (see page 85 for what these are) and concluding paragraphs at the ends.

Key ideas

The second stage is to establish what the key ideas are in a section at a time and what the author is saying about them. Follow the textbook marking advice on page 66.

Read

The third stage is to read each section to see if the author's arguments are convincing, focusing your mind on facts, ideas and how they relate. Use the author's signposting clues to follow his/her line of thinking.

Recall

The fourth stage is to recall, in outline, what you have read. You can use the textbook markings to help you.

Reflect

Fifthly, you reflect on it. You can use the questions suggested on page 63 and any others you feel are appropriate.

Review

Lastly, when you've repeated this process for a whole chapter, review what you've learned. Tie together the main points and subpoints of each individual section into a whole outline for the chapter.

If you are reading the whole book, then such review should also take place at the end, to tie together the reviews of each chapter.

Maintaining your motivation

Sometimes a subject starts to become boring, but you still need to plough on, because it is part of your course. How can you revive flagging interest? Sometimes a subject seems to be all facts and those themselves do not seem very relevant or interesting. You may think, 'I can't see where this is going', or 'I'm at a loss to see any shape or principles underlying it.'

1. Going back to basics

One remedy for this is to go back to basics; read some elementary level books on the subject, where the principles will stare you in the face. When you return to the higher level material it should make more sense to you.

2. Standing ideas on their heads

Another way to pep up your interest level is to turn concepts into their opposites. Ask if the arguments, or theories, still apply. If not, why?

3. Out-guessing the author

Try out-guessing the author. Look out for signals that he is going to draw a conclusion:

> 'Considering what evidence there is...'
> 'What this all really means is...'

Close your eyes and finish the sentence for him. Try this when you spot other signposts in the text, too, for example:

> 'On the other hand...'

There will be many opportunities in the text for you to do this, and the more familiar you are with the subject and writer the more you will succeed.

4. Working in stages

When the light at the end of the tunnel seems a long way off stop focusing on it and fix your attention upon shorter 'staging points'. Suppose you have four essays to do, seemingly impossible in the time available; focus on the half-way mark instead. If still overwhelmed, set yourself even smaller goals; think only of getting the material for the *first* essay.

Coaxing yourself along in this way you will soon reach a point where the light at the end of the tunnel is clearly visible. You may then find the energy to make a final sprint, working with vigour you would not have imagined a month or so ago.

5. Coping with study fatigue

Struggling on with scholarly work can sometimes seem like a bit of a marathon run, and a similar thing happens in both – we get weary. But have you ever heard of 'jogger's high'? All serious runners experience this. When they force their way through the barriers of fatigue they suddenly find a new source of energy, a reserve which people of average physical activity never use. This is because a brain chemical called **endorphin** is released.

What has this got to do with study fatigue? Well, the philosopher, William James wrote of something very similar to this in relation to the mind. He called it 'second wind'. If we battle on stubbornly when our mind is telling us it is fed up and wants a rest, we find we reach a new source of motivation, of will power. Before we know it we are changing up a gear. More fascinating still, he also wrote of third and fourth winds – what power, if you can harness it!

6. Turning to film and television

Look out for films and TV documentaries on your subject. These are written for a general viewership rather than for scholars and are likely to have a dash of excitement about them. Visiting relevant exhibitions and museums can breathe a breath of fresh air into a flagging relationship with your work too.

7. Varying your study method

Perhaps you are trying to do it all at once. If so, no wonder interest tends to wane. Try doing your research and gathering your notes for one essay, then move on to writing the first draft of an essay for a completely different subject. Following that, amend the first draft of an assignment for a third subject and then write up the final copy for an essay for a fourth. This way you are less likely to become bored with a task.

Managing your work like this you will be spending no more than two or three hours on each subject before moving onto something quite different. A change is as good as a rest, they say, and it certainly seems true in this respect.

Retaining the information

An average student can recall about half of what he or she has read immediately afterwards, and only about a fifth of it a fortnight later. Where fiction is concerned, it has been found that the average student can recall 86% of the key ideas in a story after an hour, and 23% of the rest.

Hardly any improvement is gained by simple re-reading. Let this be a warning to anyone who relies on simple reading and re-reading of notes prior to an exam. Re-reading a section improves retention by less than 10% – not much reward for double the effort.

The more interested we are in the material, the more we retain it. We also tend to remember arguments we agree with more than those which we don't. Focusing on principles rather than detail will also help, as will reciting after reading and frequent reviewing.

It is '*doing* something with material' which makes the mind store it permanently. The more you do with it – the more you manipulate it – the better rooted it will be in your memory and the easier it will be to recall. Reflecting, considering strengths and weaknesses of arguments, imposing 'What ifs', changing concepts to their opposite forms, and considering whether the arguments still hold true – all are ways of processing information and strengthening your memory trace.

MAKING NOTES

It is best to make your notes on loose-leaf sheets. You may want from time to time, to look at them side by side, rearrange the order, or even replace some sections with amended notes. It is wise to write on one side only for these reasons; the low cost of A4 notepads today makes this quite feasible.

Ringbinders are ideal for storing loose-leaf sheets and these are very cheap to buy these days. Sets of coloured card divider-sheets, with a choice of alphabetically or numerically ordered thumb-tabs, aid organisation of, and quick access to, material.

It is wise to write your name, course, course number and personal tutor's name on the first sheet, in case the notes should get lost. It may not be wise to include your personal address, especially if you are female, because of the risk of unwelcome callers.

Record cards are another medium for notes, especially if you are a research student. Ideas, together with the full bibliographical references and cross-references to other cards can be stored in alphabetical order in a card-index file. Neither the cards nor the containers are expensive to buy.

Effective note-taking is a very different technique to other forms of writing. There is no need to write full sentences. Brief phrases containing the main points are all that is necessary. These are called 'working notes'.

How much should you note? For most purposes a half-page per chapter or one-hour lecture is the most you should need.

You can organise note sections using indentation, numbering and underlining or highlighting. Use underlining for headings and sub-headings. Leave a margin for any future annotations. Lastly, but importantly, label the individual sections clearly, so that you can find them when you want them. It is no good having brilliant notes which you cannot find when you need them.

Writing notes

Who are you writing notes for? Who is going to read them? You, and you alone.

When we communicate, our aim is to get our message across in as short a form as possible. Every sensible person would agree that it is pointless to write more than is necessary to achieve that aim. You will not need to write anywhere near as much to communicate something to yourself when you are reading your notes over in the future, as if you had to communicate those ideas to another person. The slightest clue on paper will enable you to access more areas of the material already stored away in your mind. What on earth is the point, then, in writing all those ideas out in full? It will only lead to a waste of time in both writing and reading them, encourage a superficial treatment of the ideas (reading the matter as mere words rather than meanings), and deprive you of the chance of strengthening your memory trace by making yourself recall the material from mind.

Abbreviating information

Key words and phrases are sufficient. Furthermore, long words can be shortened, for example: 'Stats' for 'Statistics'. Standard abbreviations can be used as can also standard symbols, for example: ∴ for 'therefore'. You should develop your own personal shorthand. The more creative you are the easier this will be.

Shorthand

Some adult students, especially those who have been clerks or journalists, will have learned formal shorthand methods, such as

Pitman's shorthand schemes or Pitman's speedwriting. They will find these very useful, but it would not be a good use of time for other students to learn these from scratch for the purpose of studying another subject; you can develop your own personalised shorthand quite easily. Some of the Pitman speedwriting techniques, however, are very easy to remember and develop. Students may find them useful. These include:

c	=	ch as in chip
k	=	c as in cat or k as in kind
ʃ	=	f as in five or ph as in phase
|	=	t as in tea
t	=	th as in thought
⌒	=	m as in map
∩	=	n as in note
v	=	v as in van
⌣	=	w as in water

This is a mere fraction of the range of forms the system uses.

Using pictures
Pictures are particularly useful in note-taking. There is an old Chinese saying that one picture is worth a thousand words.

Using studygrams (spidergrams)
Another form of note-taking is the studygram (or spidergram). Instead of linear form it employs diagrammatic form. The advantage is that details of the whole subject, and all the relationships between the parts can be viewed at once. Linear notes on the other hand have to be viewed in sequence.

The studygram technique uses the right hemisphere of the brain, while linear notes use the left. It is a good idea to do your note-taking in both forms, so then you have a record in both parts of your head. Your retention and recall ability will benefit from the fact that you have to translate the linear notes into the spatial, studygram format, and vice versa. Such translation strengthens memory trace.

Another form of translation which is very useful for increasing comprehension and strengthening memory trace is successive note reduction. Reduce each section of notes to one page, then each one page to one paragraph, and so on, until you have reduced your notes for a whole subject to key points written on a single postcard.

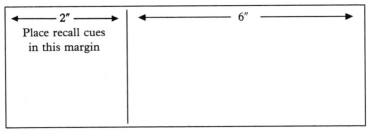

Fig. 3. Format of the 2-6 notetaking method.

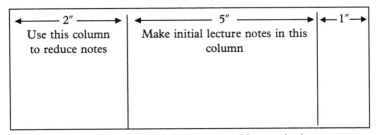

Fig. 4. Format of the 251 notetaking method.

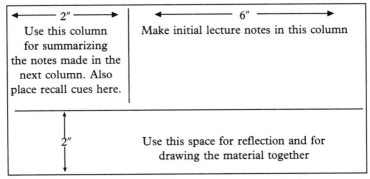

Fig. 5. Format of the 262 notetaking method.

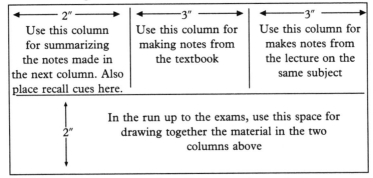

Fig. 6. Format of the 2332 notetaking method.

The wider information, and the way it relates to these key points, will have become well rooted in your memory in this process of reduction. This activity is particularly valuable close to exams.

Note-taking involves:

- recording
- reducing
- reciting
- reflecting
- reviewing

These are known as the 5 r's of note-taking.

Proven techniques
Just as advanced schemes of reading have been devised to help students study effectively, so they have of note-taking. Four different methods will be outlined on the following pages.

SUMMARY

1. Give the right impression. Foster high teacher expectations by being punctual, prepared and actively interested.

2. Estimate the teacher's treatment of the subject by comparing the course textbook with the syllabus, essay questions and past exam questions.

3. If you don't understand, say so.

4. Become a skilled library user.

5. It is a fallacy that slow reading is careful reading. Improve your reading speed.

6. Use questioning technique.

7. Look for signposts.

8. Mark your textbooks appropriately.

9. Understand the different reading techniques.

10. Understand the proven note-taking techniques.

CASE STUDIES

Tom keeps a low profile

Tom Elliot turns up at class without any idea of what is going to be dealt with. Often he doesn't understand, but he doesn't say so. He doesn't like to stand out.

Tom is not a skilled reader. He has never heard of SQ3R or OK4R techniques. He sometimes marks his own textbooks, but he ends up underlining so much that it's the bits which aren't marked that stand out. When he realises this he gives up trying to mark them at all.

Jennifer takes full advantage

Jennifer Goss realises full well that what her teacher expects of her will have a profound effect upon her achievement. As a result, Jennifer is always there on time, in the front row, saying her bit, letting the teacher know she is 'on the ball' and meaning business – letting the teacher know that his words will not fall on deaf ears so far as she is concerned.

Jennifer has made a careful comparison of all the main sources: the syllabus, textbook, past papers and essay questions. She now has a good idea of what the course is going to cover – it's all the pieces which overlap. Consequently, she is right there with well-targeted questions and comments.

Nor does she waste time when she is in the library – no browsing along shelves. She uses the computer proficiently and knows how to track down the most recent information on a subject quickly.

Jennifer reads rapidly, using the OK4R technique. She marks her material intelligently, going back and marking each section of twenty or so lines after she has read it.

Her note-taking skills are also commendable. She uses largely the 2332 technique.

Karen – a study slave

Karen Morris is always alert in class and wants to learn, but she expects the teacher to give verbatim notes. When she doesn't Karen often asks for a note to be given to the class. She writes it down as the teacher says it, sometimes asking her to 'Go slower, please.'

Karen reads slowly because she feels she may miss something otherwise. She does not use questioning techniques, she just reads things over again and again. She would be appalled at the idea of marking her textbooks. What, spoil them? She had even considered covering them.

DISCUSSION POINTS

1. How much effect on achievement do you think teacher expectations have? In what ways do they work?

2. Which of the reading techniques do you think would be best for you, and why?

3. Which of the note-taking techniques do you think would work best for you, and why?

4
Developing Your Writing Skills

THE FUNCTIONS OF ESSAYS

Many students regard essays as little more than a means of reward or punishment for effort put in, or not put in. They fail to realise the crucial role of the essay which is a means of:

- assessing the progress of knowledge and skill
- applying that knowledge and skill
- diagnosing and prescribing remedial action.

They do not think about the tutor's comments, nor consider discussing them with him/her. Very often they cannot read them, which is itself a sound reason for going to see the tutor. In the main, however, they do not do so and this is a tremendous waste of a crucial learning resource. If you do not take tutors' comments seriously and act on them, you will just go on repeating errors until they become second nature to you.

Interpreting essay questions

Many students take a rather casual approach towards interpreting essay questions, but in further and higher education this is risky. The essay questions are rarely that simple; they are designed so that students really have to think about them.

- If the question seems straightforward consider that you may well have interpreted it wrongly.

1. Begin by underlining what you feel are the key terms in the question.

2. Split up the question into its parts and bracket them off. Be sure you have noticed all the parts; each has to be dealt with separately.

3. Each of the concepts in the question has to be defined and the relationships between them dealt with.

4. Ask not only what the question is asking for, but also what it is not asking for, and make the point in the introduction to your essay. That way you are both proving you have given the question serious attention and also defending your response.

5. Ask yourself, what dimensions does the question have? What exceptions are there to any arguments suggested in it?

While you are writing the essay, keep returning to your interpretation each time you end a paragraph and start a fresh one, to make sure you are not straying off the point.

Your tutor will also want to see that an adequate number of arguments has been selected and developed (about 15 for a 2,500 word essay, about 12 for a 2,000, 9 for a 1,500 and about 5 for a 1000-word one.)

Each idea must be presented clearly and unambiguously. Use appropriate examples and include reference to evidence or authority (referencing to authority means citing the work of an acknowledged expert on the subject).

APPROACHING THE TASK

There are two fundamentally different approaches to writing an essay. They are what could be called:

- an **inductive** method – putting order on information you have collected together

- a **deductive** method – working out a response from relevant principles or theory and then finding the information to back it up.

In the first you have to organise your notes into a suitable structure; in the second you set up a skeleton of ideas and then flesh it out from your research notes.

Getting your structure right for the subject
Whichever approach you use there are two basic structures which you can choose from for most essays – a vertical structure or a lateral structure.

Vertical essay structure
The vertical structure is where the entire 'case for' is presented, then the case against, followed by a summary and conclusion.

Lateral essay structure
A lateral structure, instead, takes each argument in turn together with the counter arguments, point-for-point for, point-for-point against, and so on. This one tends to be favoured by social scientists, for example psychologists, sociologists, geographers, business studies scholars, political scientists, and economists.

Descriptive essays
Descriptive essays are a different kettle of fish. They do not necessarily lend themselves to either of these structures.

WRITING THE ESSAY

Building effective arguments
Building effective arguments involves the following:

- defining concepts being used

- setting firm foundations on which to base your reasoning

- using logical reasoning to build up a case

- elaborating your arguments in different ways

- using appropriate examples

- presenting appropriate evidence

- considering every angle

- acknowledging the challenges and overcoming them in advance.

Whatever you do, avoid **plagiarism**. That is the use of other people's ideas without attributing them to those people. The way to avoid this is explained later in a section on referencing and bibliographies (see page 88).

Keep to the point; it is very easy to stray. If you feel that going off on a tangent is justified, defend your decision to do so.

Always keep your intended audience in mind when you write. You can then use appropriate language and level of explanation for them. Who is it you are writing for? In general, assume your reader to have no special knowledge of the subject, but has sufficient intelligence to understand your arguments if you explain them clearly.

Punctuating correctly

Proficiency in punctuation is often lacking among further and higher education students. Here is a brief guide to standard methods:

Symbol	Name	Where to use
.	Full stop	At the end of sentence or after abbreviation.
,	Comma	Natural pause. Enclosing personal names in speech. Enclosing words in apposition, *eg* 'Jane, my flat-mate, will be at home.' Words like however, then, thus, hence and therefore. Separating direct from indirect speech, eg. 'I've finished my essay,' said John. Separating items in a list, *eg* We need: flour, margarine, milk, sugar and an egg.
;	Semi-colon	For use where the ideas contained in two potential sentences are so close in meaning that it warrants joining them into one sentence. At each side of the semi-colon there must be all the elements of a complete sentence.
:	Colon	Before a list, example or elaboration.
( )	Brackets	Use where you are including something which is not syntactically an essential part of the sentence, but merely gives extra information about the subject. Example: David (the one who had found the notes) did the same course last year, so he knew they must belong to someone in that class.
?	Question mark	For questions.

!	Exclamation mark	Use to indicate exclamations (do not over-use this one).
'	Apostrophe	Use: Where there are missing letters. To indicate possession, *eg* Jane's car.
-	Hyphen	To join two words into a compound word, *eg* water-mill. To join two halves of a word on separate lines (only at the end of a complete syllable, though), eg Never 'Mo-untain' but Moun-tain' is acceptable. The hyphen should always go at the end of the line, never at the beginning.
–	Dash	Slightly larger than the hyphen, used to indicate faltering speech, *eg* Well – er – I – er – Where there is a sudden break in speech, *eg* 'Are you going on holiday this – Oh, there's the doorbell.'
" and "	Speech marks	To enclose speech in the text, though the modern style is increasingly to use single commas. In the event of speech within speech, use the double speech marks for the outer speech and single speech-marks for the inner speech, eg "Well," said Rosy, "Graham came over and said 'How do you do?' to me."
' and '	Inverted commas	For highlighting particular words or phrases, for special attention.

Avoiding incomplete sentences

It is surprising how many essays are handed in – even at university – which contain incomplete sentences. Remember, sentences must have a **verb** or verb phrase (an action word or phrase like 'smiled', 'will run' or 'is carrying'), and a **subject** (someone, or something, doing the action). They often have an **object** too (the object of the action) eg 'is carrying a bag.'

Writing good sentences and paragraphs
Sentences should be neither too long nor too short. Vary the lengths; this knits the language together.

There are two basic types of paragraph.

- the topic sentence style

- the implicit theme style

Using topic sentences
In the topic sentence style the first sentence tells what the paragraph is about. The remaining sentences give the information promised in the first sentence.

A useful structure is to begin with a topic sentence and elaborate in a second sentence, perhaps by saying it in a different way, or using an example. Then present evidence to back the statement up and, finally, perhaps, say how it contributes to the case being built up.

The implicit theme style
The implicit theme style paragraph does not tell what the paragraph is about in the first sentence. Instead, the meaning tends to become clear as the paragraph as a whole is read. This style suits fiction writing or descriptive essays, where the language itself is intended to create an impression. The topic sentence paragraph is more appropriate for 'factual' and 'debate' type essays, where your job is to make it as easy as possible for the reader to extract the information.

Using a dictionary
As you write, keep to hand a good dictionary, for example *The Concise Oxford Dictionary*, or *The Oxford Reference Dictionary*. A thesaurus, too, will be of great help. This is a book of *synonyms* and *antonyms*. In English usage we avoid using the same word twice in the same part of the text, so a thesaurus can save us a lot of time. A third useful aid to have to hand is a guide to English usage.

Be legible
If you are writing your essays in longhand be careful to make your handwriting legible. Your marks are not likely to depend on its appearance, but you will not receive marks for ideas your tutor cannot read. If your writing is too bad you may be asked to do it again.

Writing good introductions and summaries
An acceptable way of writing introductions is:

Sentence 1
A general statement which outlines the case being made in the essay.

Sentence 2
Present the list of arguments to be used and the order in which they will appear.

Sentence 3
Mention any conclusion which will be drawn.

Sentence 4
If the subject is a value charged one, for example privatisation of the health service, it is a mark of academic integrity for the writer to declare his or her own personal feelings on the question. We all have deeply held feelings about things: we cannot avoid them. They are not entirely based on reason. Nevertheless, they can influence the way we select evidence, the weight we place upon it and how we generally interpret it. It is right and proper to declare our value standpoints so that readers can take this into account when they are evaluating the cases we are making.

If you have an abundance of ideas, more than you can actually use within the word limit, it is a good idea to keep one paragraph, immediately before the summary, to briefly list all those ideas you would have liked to have used had you had the space.

An acceptable way to write a summary and conclusion is to list the arguments 'for and against', synthesise the material, and draw a conclusion briefly explaining how you arrived at it.

In addition, state any weaknesses or limitations of the work for example: 'This work does not take account of very recent studies in this area, the reports of which are not yet widely available in libraries', or 'This treatment of the subject does not take account of the important work by Smith (1989), which, unfortunately, could not be obtained within the available time-scale.'

KEEPING TO THE WORD LIMIT

Tutors vary in the importance they attach to word limits, but writing in a concise way is a skill which students should in any case set out to master. Some students think they should be praised rather than penalised for writing more than the word limit. They think it shows they have dealt with more material. They are wrong. Tutors find it is excess verbiage that makes their essays exceed the word limit, not excess ideas. There is an old Chinese proverb about a man who wrote a long letter because he did not have time to write a short one. Being concise is not an easy task; it requires effort and skill.

There are two other things to say about keeping to the word limit.

1. Many an average essay becomes a good one when the words make full us of the word limit, and many a good essay becomes excellent.

2. If one student presents nine important ideas in an essay written to a word limit of 1,500 words, while another includes ten ideas, but made no effort to stick to the word limit, it would be unfair to reward the second student for his/her extra idea. When a word limit is imposed it should be rigidly enforced; there should be no half measures.

Sticking to the word limit is likely to involve some unhappy decisions. When every one of your ideas seems important how can you possibly omit one of them? You may have to, though. It will force you to make fine distinctions about their relative importance.

Making a word count
Count the words. If you have written the essay longhand and your handwriting is fairly consistent, then you can count the words on one page and multiply by the number of pages (and fractions of a page). If you have typed your essay the same will apply. If you have used a computer or word processor you will be able to do a word count through your program. Calculate the excess words as a percentage of the total number of words in the essay. Example:

$$\frac{\text{Excess words} \quad \times 100}{\text{Total number of words}}$$

Assuming the level of excess is consistent throughout your writing, in most cases a reasonable assumption, you can expect to have to cut about that percentage from each and every paragraph. This is not a rigid rule, but it will give you an idea of the size of your task.

You can calculate the expected word-cut in terms of pages, half-pages, or even paragraphs. This will give you some guide as to how your word-cutting is progressing. It will enable you to set little word-cutting goals, which will feel easier than facing the bewildering task of cutting a percentage of words from the whole essay.

1. First, look for repetition of the same ideas. Remove such duplications.

2. Second, look at each individual sentence to see if the word usage could be reduced. Are there words in the sentences serving no useful purpose? Some of the adjectives and/or adverbs could, perhaps, be removed. Are there places where you could use one word in place of two or three?

When all these possibilities have been exhausted if there are still significantly too many words you must evaluate the sub-points and even the main points you have used. Say to yourself, 'I don't want to lose any of these ideas, but if something has to go which should it be?' The decision will be an unhappy one, but it has to be made. If you have kept one paragraph, immediately before the summary, for briefly listing ideas which you would have liked to have included if you had had the space then you can add to it the ideas you are having to discard from the main treatment.

REFERENCING YOUR WORK

Tutors vary in the importance they place on good bibliographies and referencing.

However, undergraduates at least should be learning to write in a professional way. They must master the conventional techniques of referencing and writing bibliographies. Furthermore, without proper referencing it is difficult, if not impossible, for your tutor to check the accuracy of your reporting, citing and quoting.

Everything claimed as fact or theory in an essay should be supported by reference to evidence or authority (the book, article, or report from which the information was taken).

It is an established convention that academics who discover facts or develop theories and publish them before anyone else shall be entitled to regard them as their own **intellectual property**; anyone who uses them should acknowledge the right of the intellectual property owners. They do this by writing the person's name and year of publication after the ideas, theories or facts when they, themselves, use them in a text. They also write a full reference to the work at the end of the essay, or book.

Three styles of referencing

Three alternative styles of referencing are in common use:

1. To place in the text, immediately after the idea used, the author's name, year of publication (and page number if a verbatim quote is being used). Example: (Smith, 1989, p.23). Write Smith 1989b if it was the second work of that year by that same author being used in the same essay.

2. A superscript number referring to a footnote giving the writer's name, year of publication and page number. Example: 'the world is running out of ice cream'.[1]

Footnotes:
1. Smith (1989) p. 3.

---

3. A superscript number referring to a set of notes consecutively numbered throughout the whole text, placed at the end of the essay, just before the bibliography.

Compiling bibliographies

The full reference to each work is then given in the bibliography. Some people head the list 'References' instead. There are rigid conventions regarding the presentation of this. There are two alternative styles. Only the one regarded as most common will be given here, though.

The normal style

It should be written as shown in the following example:

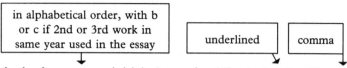

1. Author's surname, initials (year of publication) <u>title of book,</u>
town of publication:Publisher's name

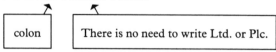

2. If the work is an article then the record is as follows:

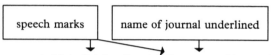

Author's surname, initials "title of article", <u>name of journal</u>,
volume number, date of publication.

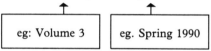

3. If there are more than two authors for one work, for example
Jones, Smith and Adams, the convention is to list them as
Jones et al.

4. It is conventional to start only the first word in the title with a
capital letter, not each word.

5. It is not conventional to indent, such as

Smith (1990)   <u>The most important finding in the world</u>
                Harmondsworth:Penguin
Edwards (1994)<u>Studying after a night out</u>, London:
                Harrison and Swan.

The acceptable format would be:

Smith (1990) <u>The most important finding in the world,</u>
Harmondsworth:Penguin

Edwards (1994) <u>Studying after a night out</u>, London: Harrison
and Swan.

MAKING A FINAL CHECK

Before you hand the essay in have one final look over it.

- Does it make sense?

- Does it sound alright read aloud?

- Is the meaning clear in all the paragraphs?

- Are your facts right?

- Is the grammar right?

- Should you change the order of words in any of the sentences?

- Is the spelling and punctuation OK?

- Have you used the right words?

- Have you used too many words?

- Are the sentences long and rambling?

- Do the sentences seem short and abrupt?

- Do the sentence lengths vary?

Ask someone else to read it. If a reasonably intelligent person without knowledge of your subject cannot understand what you are talking about, then it needs further attention before you hand it in. The aim is to communicate your ideas, not to blind the reader with science.

Time check

How much time should you allow for writing an essay? On the average students can expect to spend about 15 hours on a 2,500 word essay and pro-rata for other word-lengths.

SUMMARY

1. Essays are both a means of assessment and a learning resource.

2. Interpret questions carefully; they are often not as straightforward as they at first seem.

3. Two alternative approaches to essay writing are 'placing a structure on material' and 'placing material in a structure'.

4. Essays can be structured vertically or laterally.

5. Write with a target audience in mind.

6. Master the rules of grammar, punctuation and spelling.

7. Paragraphs can be of 'topic sentence' or 'implicit themes'.

8. Master the techniques of writing good introductions and summaries.

9. Master the art of referencing and writing bibliographies.

10. Take word-limits seriously.

CASE STUDIES

Tom's weaknesses

Tom Elliot's approach to essay writing is a mainly deductive one. He works out basically what he wants to say in his head. He then structures the essay, and finds material to put into it. He tends to use vertical structures; it seems logical to him to give the 'case for' followed by the 'case against', then summing up and concluding.

English is not Tom's strong point. His referencing and bibliographical techniques leave a lot to be desired, too. The latter tend to be mere lists of books he has used without any real standardisation of presentation.

Jenny succeeds

Jennifer Goss really excels when it comes to writing. She realises the value of essays – both a means of assessment and a learning resource. She interprets questions carefully and has taught herself to mistrust any interpretation which seems straightforward. She uses both inductive and deductive approaches, though mostly the former. The structures she uses are almost invariably lateral ones.

Imagining her reader as an intelligent lay-person, she writes sensitively with the comprehension needs of such a reader in mind. Her spelling, punctuation and grammar are impeccable. She writes skilful and useful introductions and summaries. She has mastered referencing and bibliographical techniques. Her attention to word limits is rigorous. It's no wonder her work attracts top marks every time.

Karen has yet to understand

To Karen Morris, essays are simply a routine of rewards and admonishments. She interprets questions very superficially. Her approach is to ask other students how they intend to set about the task. Karen sees no need to explain all her ideas in detail. After all, her teacher gave her the ideas she is using, so surely he will understand and accept them when he reads the essay. She cannot see why she needs to spell them out.

As for word limits, it seems illogical to her that a student should be penalised for writing too much. When she does exceed the word limits, Karen argues that there is simply no way she could cut the words down. Karen tends to be awarded rather low marks in her essays.

DISCUSSION POINTS

1. Do you approach your own essay writing by placing a structure on material, or placing material in a structure? Why do you tend to choose your preferred method?

2. Do you prefer to structure essays vertically or laterally? Why do you prefer this method?

3. How important do you think referencing and bibliographies are?

5
Developing Your Quantitative Skills

CHECKING YOUR SKILLS

Basic arithmetic skills

Just about everyone knows how to add, subtract, multiply and divide. However, many mature students entering higher education are a little rusty on, and sometimes have never covered, **fractions**, **percentages**, and **decimals**. Nor is this limited to mature students, who have been out of compulsory schooling for some time; many young people in further and higher education also have difficulties in these areas. Perhaps maths was just not a subject which fired them with enthusiasm at school.

Averages

When it comes to **averages** and other simple statistics, the proportion of people who lack skills is even greater. Yet many will need these skills in further and higher education.

Graphs and charts

Many lack the skills of interpreting information from **graphs** and **charts**. Nor can they translate information from this form of presentation to the more straightforward quantitative form.

Simple equations

Many people do not know how to solve even simple **equations**, yet this is one of the most powerful problem-solving methods we have. It is important to begin to develop skills in this area and it is hoped this chapter will help you do so.

Even those beginning higher education with maths A-level under their belts can improve their maths skills (with a little understanding of metacognitive knowledge thinking patterns) and it is on this subject which this chapter ends.

USING SYMBOLS

Everybody knows the four basic symbols $+$, $-$, $\div$ and $\times$. But do you know what $\sum$ and $\simeq$ mean?

A basic user's guide

Here is a list of symbols you are likely to come across together with their meanings:

$+$	plus
$-$	minus
$\div$	divide
$\times$	multiply
$=$	equals
$\simeq$	approximately equal to
$\equiv$	identical to
$<$	less than
$>$	greater than
$\leqslant$	is less than or equal to
$\geqslant$	is greater than or equal to
$\neq$	is not equal to
$\pm$	plus or minus
$\sum$	the sum of
$\sim$	the difference between a and b
$\mid$	when
1	index number, or exponent. (It could be any number)
1	subscripts (used to label groups of quantities in the sequence. It could be any number).

WORK FAST – WORK ACCURATELY

Working fast actually aids accuracy; working slow has the opposite effect. For an explanation of why this is so refer back to page 14.

Using approximations

You can greatly reduce the risk of arithmetical slips by approximating your answer. You should get into the habit of always doing this.

Example: addition

When you are making a rough estimate of what two numbers added together make, you can round one up and the other down to make things easy. The amount to round by depends on the size of the figure. For example, if you are adding 22 and 87 you could round the 22 down to 20, and the 87 up to 90. Or, if you are adding 2,900 and 1,100 it would reasonable to round up and down by 100, in other words to 3,000 and 1,000.

Multiplying
The same applies when you are multiplying. This is particularly valuable where there are decimals involved, because it enables you to spot immediately if you have placed the decimal point in the wrong place in your answer.

Using 'orders of magnitude'
Another way of approximating is to use **order of magnitude** estimates. To do this you divide figures by 10, 100, 1000 , *etc.*, to make them easier to handle. Conversely, you multiply them by 10 if they are very small numbers like 0.0006. For example 300 x 150 can be reduced to 3 x 1.5; then the 4 decimal places you removed from the two figures together can be put back into your answer so that it is not 4.5 but 45,000.

Checking your answers
Always check your answer and try to do so in a different way to the one in which you calculated it. For example, when you *subtract* one figure from another, check your answer by *adding* it back on to make sure you arrive at your original figure.

Example
$$320 -$$
$$\underline{110}$$
$$210 +$$
$$\underline{110}$$
$$320$$

DOING ARITHMETIC

Positive and negative numbers
Most people know how to handle simple addition and subtraction, but what about where **positive** and **negative** numbers (numbers with a minus sign before them) are concerned? It can be confusing. All you do is take the smaller from the larger and use the sign of the larger.

For example, if you are adding a positive 2 to a negative 4 it goes like this:

$$-4+2 = -2$$

All we have really done is to rearrange the order so, that it can be carried out in the simple subtraction way.

All numbers are actually 'signed', either with '+' or '−' before them. But if it is the first number in a line, and the sign is a +, we do not bother to write it. In other words, $2-1$ is strictly speaking $+2-1$. We just don't need to write in the plus before the first number.

Let's consider a multiple addition and subtraction problem like this:

$$3-6+1-2$$

All we do is collect all the positive terms and add them together, and then collect all the negative terms and add them together. We then take the smaller from the larger and use the sign of the larger. Using the above example:

$$[+3] \text{ and } [+1] \text{ is } [+4]$$
$$[-6] \text{ and } [-2] \text{ is } [-8]$$
$$[-8] \text{ and } [+4] \text{ is } [-4]$$

The brackets are used here just to make things clear. You would not normally use them in such a calculation.

The more we practise adding and subtracting the easier it becomes. Have you noticed how outstandingly quick darts players are at adding and subtracting? True, their skill may be partly limited to the combinations of scores which occur in a darts game, but it demonstrates the point that practice increases skill.

Multiplication

Here are a few basic facts about multiplication:

- Multiplying or dividing a number by 1 leaves it unchanged.

- Multiplying a number by 0 will give zero. Examples: $8 \times 0 = 0$. $147.72 \times 0 = 0$.

- Any number divided by itself equals 1, except where 0 is concerned.

- You cannot divide 0 by anything. If mathematics allowed this it would lead to absurdity for we would be able to create something from nothing, for example: $0 \div 0 = 1$. Therefore,

$$\frac{0}{0} + \frac{0}{0} = 2$$

Reciprocals

The reciprocal of a number is that number divided into 1. For example: The reciprocal of 4 is ¼. Dividing by a number is the same thing as multiplying by its reciprocal. For example:

$$8 \div 4 = 8 \times \frac{1}{4}$$

Managing numbers with unlike signs

People are often confused about multiplying and dividing numbers with unlike signs, for example: $3 \times (-4)$. The rule is when multiplying 'like' signs (-3×-4, or $+3 \times +4$) the answer is always positive ($+12$). But if you are multiplying 'unlike' signs ($+3 \times -4$) the answer is always negative (-12).

- Remember: like signs give positive numbers. Unlike signs give negative ones.

What if there are more than two terms – for example: $2 \times 6 \times (-3)$. The rule is that if there is an equal number of positive and negative terms the answer will be positive (but if not, negative). Examples:

$$2 \times 3 \times (-3) = -18, \text{ but } 2 \times 3 \times (-3) \times (-2) = 36.$$

Using indices

Indices (little figures written at the top right-hand corner of a figure) indicate that the number is to be multiplied by itself that many times. For example: 3^5 equals $3 \times 3 \times 3 \times 3 \times 3$.

When multiplying figures with indices all you need to do is add the indices. For example:

$$3^2 \times 3^3 = 3^5$$

Dividing is the reverse you subtract them. For example:

$$3^5 \div 3^2 = 3^3$$

Sometimes you are asked to multiply the actual indices. When this is so it is written like this:

$$(5^3)^3 = 5^9$$

A number raised to the 2nd power we call the **square** of that number. For example, the square of 4 is 16:

$$4^2 = 16$$

When raised to the 3rd power we call it the cube. For example 4 cubed is:

$$4^3 = 64$$

If a number has an index number of -1 it means the reciprocal of that number. Example:

$$3^{-1} \text{ is } {}^1/_3$$

Square roots and cubic roots

An index number can even be a fraction, for example $9^{1/2}$. This means a **root** of that number. An index number of $^{1/2}$ means the **square root**; an index number of $^{1/3}$ means the **cubic root.**

- A square root of a number is that which if squared would result in that number. Example: The square root of 4 is 2 ($2 \times 2 = 4$).

- A cubic root is that which if cubed would result in it. Example: the cubic root of 27 is 3 ($3 \times 3 \times 3 = 27$).

Multiplying or dividing by 10 is an absolute doddle. Yet it is surprising how many people do not know this. I watched a Post Office counter clerk multiplying by 10 on a calculator and could hardly believe my eyes. To multiply by 10 all you do is add a nought. Or, if there are decimal places, you move the point one place to the right. To divide by 10 you do the reverse. Examples:

$$10 \times 90 = 900 \qquad 90 \div 10 = 9$$
$$10 \times 72.45 = 724.5 \qquad 72.45 \div 10 = 7.245$$

Even though we have calculators today the value of learning basic multiplication tables is unquestionable. If you do not know them learn them. When you have learned each one, learn to say it backwards. Then start in the middle and work forwards to the end and backwards to the beginning. Then start a quarter of the way through and do likewise and then three-quarters of the way in. Get somebody to test you and keep working at it until you are absolutely sure you can give an immediate answer to any multiplication question up to 12×12. Schools do not always deal with this today, but they have other, more complicated, procedures to deal with; learning tables is something you can do for yourself.

Order of arithmetic operations

Many people are unsure how to handle complex calculations — multi-part problems containing more than one symbol. For example:

$$3 \times 4 + 5 - 6 \div 7$$

Do the brackets and roots first

If there are any bracketed parts of the problem these should be dealt with first. What you do here is apply the term outside the brackets to every value inside them, for example:

$$3(a + b) \text{ becomes } 3a + 3b$$

Everything underneath a radical (root) sign, such as $\sqrt{}$, is dealt with in this way, too, as if bracketed. The same applies to what is below or above the line in a fraction.

Next do any multiplication ($\times$) and division ($\div$) parts of the calculation.

In complex expressions (containing several different symbols) adding and subtracting is done last and the order in which these two are performed does not matter. After all, they both really amount to the same thing, subtraction being merely adding negative numbers, for example $8 - 6$ is simple $(+8)$ and (-6).

Doing fractions

If you multiply or divide both the top (the **numerator**) and the bottom (the **denominator**) the value of a fraction remains unchanged, for example:

$$\frac{1 \times 2}{2 \times 2} = \frac{2}{4} \text{ and } \frac{2 \div 2}{4 \div 2} = \frac{1}{2}$$

(The only exception is if you multiply by zero, and this procedure is not permitted in arithmetic.)

Reducing the quantities
This allows us to reduce the quantities involved in a division, so that it is easier to do. Example:

$$\frac{4,500}{500} \text{ divide both top and bottom by 100} = \frac{45}{5} \quad \text{Easy!}$$
(ie knock off two 0s)

If letters are involved: $\frac{5a}{25a}$. Divide both top and bottom by 'a' to cancel out the 'a'; this leaves $\frac{5}{25}$. Then divide both parts by 5 to leave $\frac{1}{5}$.

Multiplying and dividing fractions
To multiply fractions just multiply both the top and bottom parts. Examples:

$$\frac{1}{2} \times \frac{2}{3} = \frac{2}{6}$$

To divide fractions simply turn the second one upside down, and multiply. Example:

$$\frac{1}{2} \div \frac{2}{3} = \frac{1}{2} \times \frac{3}{2} = \frac{3}{4}$$

Adding and subtracting fractions
Contrary to what you might expect, adding and subtracting fractions is not as simple as multiplying or dividing. To add or subtract fractions you have to find the **lowest common multiple** (LCM). This is the largest number which each of the two denominators will divide into without remainder. Example:

$$\frac{1}{2} + \frac{2}{3}$$

The LCM of the two denominators here is 6, as both 2 and 3 go into it without remainder.

This becomes the bottom part (**denominator**) of the answer fraction. You then place the plus or minus sign above this. Then calculate two new **numerators** (top parts of the fraction) by dividing each of the old denominators into the new common denominator; multiply the answer in each case by the old numerators. This will give you the two new numerators. Example:

| 2 into 6 goes 3. | $\dfrac{3+4}{6}$ | 3 into 6 goes 2 |
| Multiply by 1 | | Multiply by 2 |

Then you simply add or subtract the two numerators as appropriate to arrive at the answer. Example:

$$\frac{3+4}{6}=\frac{7}{6}$$

You then have to make sure it is expressed in its lowest terms by checking whether any number will divide into both top and bottom without remainder. If this is possible it should be done, and done again, until it is no longer possible. Thus, if the denominator is greater than the numerator divide it into it.

$$7 \div 6 = 1\tfrac{1}{6}$$

Factors

A number which will divide into another number without remainder is called a factor of that number. For example, 7 is a factor of 28. There are easy ways of discovering whether a number is a factor of another number. Here are the secrets:

2   is a factor of a number if it is an even number.

3   is a factor of a number if it is a factor of its digits added together. For example, 3 must be a factor of 321 because it is a factor of 6 $(3+2+1)$.

4   is a factor of a number if it is a factor of the last two digits. For example, 4 must be a factor of 324 because it divides equally into 24.

5   is a factor of a number if it ends with 5 or 0.

9   is a factor of a number if it is a factor of its digits added together (same as 3).

10 is a factor of a number if it ends in 0.

11 is a factor of a number if the digits in the even positions add up to the same figure as the digits in the odd positions. Example: we can be sure that 11 will divide equally into 2,365 because the digits in the odd places add up to the same number as those in the even places $2+6=8$ and $3+5=8$.

Handling percentages

Expressing something as a 'percentage' is simply expressing it as a fraction with a denominator of 100, although it is not written as a fraction is normally written. Example: 75% is really 75/100.

To state a number as a percentage of a larger number we just divide the smaller number by the larger one and multiply by 100 (and to multiply by 100 you just move the decimal point two places to the right). Example: 6 as a percentage of 8 is:

$$
\begin{array}{r}
0.75 \\
8\ \overline{)6.0} \\
\underline{5.6} \\
0.40
\end{array}
\qquad \times 100 = 75\%
$$

Handling decimals

When you are adding or subtracting numbers with decimal numbers just keep all the decimal points in a vertical line even in the answer box. Example:

$$
\begin{array}{r}
8.5 \\
-\ 3.2 \\
\hline
5.3
\end{array}
$$

To multiply with decimal places ignore the decimal point while you multiply. Then count the number of decimal places in both of the original numbers together; place the decimal point in the answer that number of places from the right. For example:

DEALING WITH AVERAGES

Many people think an average is a useful generalisation about a set of circumstances. If the average salary among 10,000 people was reported to be £6,760 many would think that this gives a pretty good idea of the level of income for the members of this population. But while it could mean that each person earns around £6,760 it could *also* mean that 100 earn £200,000 while 9,900 earn £4,808. For example:

$$£$$

$$100 \times £200,000 \quad = \quad 20,000,000$$
$$9900 \times £4,808 \quad = \quad \underline{47,600,000}$$
$$67,600,000 \div 10,000 = £6,760$$

Means, medians and modes

It depends *what* average is being used. There is more than one kind:

- the mean
- the median
- the mode.

We have to ask, which is being used? Is it the most useful in the circumstances?

Example 1
If a small number of people were earning high salaries and most were earning low ones then the most useful kind of average would be the *mode*. This is simply the most frequently occurring figure. In the above example the mode would be £4,808.

Example 2
In other cases the mode could give a misleading impression. For example: if 100 people earned £200,000 and the remaining 9,900 all earned different, but much lower, amounts the modal average would be £200,000. However, this would bear no resemblance to what most people were earning.

The mean
The mean (or arithmetic mean, as it is often called) is all the values added together and then divided by the number of values in the calculation.

The median
The median is simply the middle number in a series. Example: if five people had salaries of £6,000, £8,000, £10,000, £12,000 and £14,000 respectively, the median salary would be £10,000. If there are two middle numbers, for example, in a series of 6 values, add them together and divide by 2.

Standard deviation and range
One good way to tell whether an average is the most suitable is to ask what the **range** is (between the smallest and the largest values) and what the **standard deviation** is (basically the average deviation from the average). The smaller the range and standard deviation the more useful the average.

Using the above example, if the average salary in a population of 10,000 people was reported to be £6,760, but the standard deviation from the mean was £2,000, then the average would not really be telling you anything useful. However, if the standard deviation was only £300 it would be quite a meaningful average.

GRAPHS, CHARTS AND PICTOGRAMS

Information can be presented in text, numerical tables or diagrams. One of the most common diagram types is the graph.

Using graphs
The essential information to look for in a graph is the slope and shape of the line. A straight, or more or less straight, line is known as a **linear trend**. As well as having to read information from graphs you will also need to learn how to present information in this way. In fact, it is important for you to practise translating between one form and another. When you come across important information in tabular form, draw a graph of it and vice versa. Try also to express the information in words.

The components of a graph
The horizontal plane of a graph is known as the **abscissa**, but is often referred to as the **x axis**. The vertical plane is the **ordinate**, but is often referred to as the **y axis**. You can remember which is which by picturing the vertical (or more or less vertical) line in the letter y itself, but not in the letter x. Small letters are used for these.

The point where the x and y axes meet is known as the **origin**, usually labelled O.

Plotting the variables

You may be unsure which of your variables to use the x axis for and which the y. The answer is use the x for the **independent variable** and the y for the **dependent variable**. But which is the independent variable and which the dependent one? The independent variable is the one you wish to show is causing a change in the other variable. For example, you could have 'hours spent studying' plotted along the x axis, and different achievement levels plotted up the y axis.

Converting graphs to equations

You may need to convert the information in a straight line graph to an algebraic equation. Begin with noting where the line cuts the y axis – this is the **c value** of the equation. Then decide what the relationship is between the x and y values at each point along the lines.

Translating graph information into algebraic form and vice versa

The slope of a line, and the point at which it cuts through the y axis, are both expressed by the equation $y = mx + c$. Here y is the measurement on the y axis, m is the number of times it is greater than or smaller than the measurement along the x axis and c is the point on the y axis at which the trend line cuts through the y axis. Suppose each point along the graph line is such that it has gone up three times as much as it has moved along the horizontal plane. The coefficient (multiplier) of x is 3. If the c value were 1 then the resulting equation would be $y = 3x + 1$.

The coefficient of x represents the slope of the line. Example: If it is 2 the slope is 2 in 1. Knowing this, you will be able to practise the equations of a straight line every time you see a steep hill sign on the side of the road.

The c value may be zero, in which case there is no need to express it at all; the equation is merely $y = mx$ where m stands for any numerical value. A useful way of remembering this is by thinking of c for cut (the point at which the line cuts the y axis). An example is given in figure 7.

Sometimes the m value will be a negative number (a number with a minus sign before it). If it is, it simply means the y measurements are that many times less than the x measurements. An example is shown in figure 8.

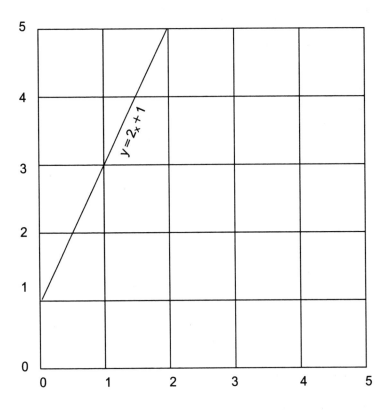

Fig. 7. Example of a linear trend line. Note that at each point the y measurement is twice the x (hence y = 2x) and the line cuts the y axis at 1 (hence + 1).

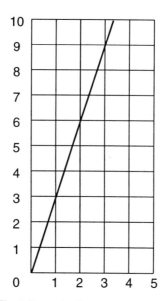

Fig. 8. Example of the trend line . y=3x.

The equation $y = x^2$ is an exponential curve. When plotting each point (each pair of co-ordinates) on the graph, the y measurement will always be the square of the x measurement. An example is given in figure 9.

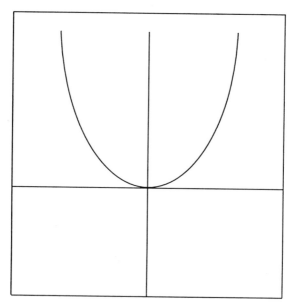

Fig. 9. Example of a trend line for the equation $y = x^2$.

Charts

Charts are another way of plotting quantitative information. **Pie charts** are useful for showing quantities as a percentage of the whole, for they appear as 'slices of the cake'.

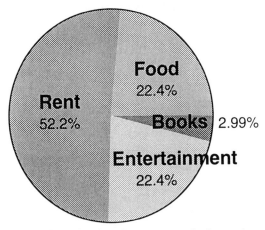

Fig. 10. A pie chart showing the way a particular student
spends his income.

Another kind of chart is the **bar chart**. The y values of different units along the x axis are shown as bars.

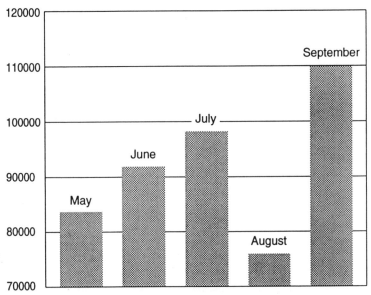

Fig. 11. Example of a bar chart showing monthly sales figures.

Pictograms

These serve the same basic purpose as bar charts, but the information in them can mislead and can be used to exaggerate claims. Instead of bars pictures are used. Consequently, when they increase vertically they increase horizontally too, in proportion. Increases and decreases thus look much greater than they would in a bar chart. Consider the example in figure 12.

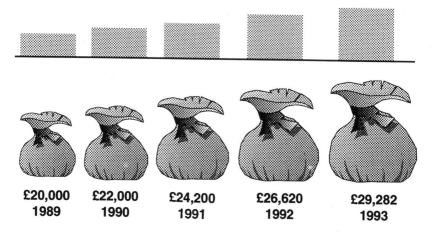

| £20,000 | £22,000 | £24,200 | £26,620 | £29,282 |
| 1989 | 1990 | 1991 | 1992 | 1993 |

Fig. 12. Example of a pictogram and bar chart side by side, showing the same information, ie wage rises of 10% per annum over 4 years.

Study all scientific diagrams carefully: the authors are unlikely to include details which are not important to the point being made.

SOLVING EQUATIONS

The basic rule for solving an equation is that whatever you do to one side you must also do to the other. There is also an order in which we proceed.

1. Remove brackets first. To do this we apply the term immediately before the brackets to everything inside them (see page 100).

2. The next thing is to remove fractions, if there are any. You do this by multiplying each side of the equation by the lowest common multiple of the original denominators. For example:

$$\frac{x}{2} - 4 = \frac{x}{5} + 8 \quad \text{(Multiply)} \qquad 5x - 4 = 2x + 8$$

both sides by 10
to give

3. Then collect all the unknown terms on one side of the equals sign. Do this by applying the same figure to both sides. If you want to move −4 across the equals sign add 4 to both sides. For example:

$$5x = 2x + 8 + 4$$

This cancels it out on one side and puts it on the other side with a changed sign. If you forget this just remember that you can move anything across the equals sign if you change its sign.

4. We now have to move the x term across the equals sign to join the other one. Do this by taking 2x away from both sides to leave:

$$5x - 2x = 8 + 4$$

5. The next stage is to simplify the values of the known terms. For example:

$$3x = 12$$

6. Finally, divide by the coefficient of the last remaining unknown term to find out what value that term itself has. For example:

$$3x = 12 \qquad \therefore \frac{3x}{3} = \frac{12}{3} \qquad \therefore x = 4$$

CHECKLIST FOR SOLVING PROBLEMS

Mathematics can be very useful in problem solving in many areas. Here is a checklist of steps to take.

1. Decide what kind of problem it is.

2. Make sure you spot every concept in the problem.

3. Decide whether you understand the concepts and theories involved. If not, read up on them.

4. Consider whether you know of any other problems of this kind which are easier to solve.

5. Substitute numbers for variables where possible.

6. Brainstorm for ideas, knowledge and connections with other problems which may help you solve it.

7. Order the brainstorming ideas you have collected by drawing in lines of connection.

8. Talk the problem over with others.

9. Use algorithms (flow charts of procedure) to clarify your thinking and guide your actions.

10. Split the problem up into smaller pieces.

11. Start at each end of the problem, work through the sub-tasks involved and try to meet in the middle. This sometimes works where problems seem otherwise too difficult.

12. Re-state the problem in a different way to see if that makes things clearer.

13. Use the power of your unconscious mind, sleep on the problem and let the answer incubate.

Thinking styles

People have habitual thinking styles. Most tend to be relatively 'left-brain' (sequential) in nature; others have relatively 'right-brain' styles. Right brain thinking is rather spatial, seeing all the bits of the problem there in front of you at once, rather than sequentially following a line of logic to arrive at your answer. If the problem seems insoluble try adopting a thinking style you would not normally use.

Elegance

One of the main guiding principles of mathematical problem solving is what is often called **Occum's razor**. The solutions to problems must be trimmed to a concise form. It is often best to leave time to spare after solving a problem and then go back to it to see if you can make the solution any more concise. This is known as the principle of elegance.

   This is precisely the value of published model answers. If these are available, as indeed they are for most A level courses, you will be selling yourself short if you do not purchase a copy.

SOME FINAL TIPS

- Try to discover the **principles** involved in different areas of mathematical problem solving.

- Try to remember the kinds of **errors** you habitually make, so that you can be on the look-out for them.

- Use **mnemonics** to remember processes, for example: acronyms. A common example of this is the mnemonic for the 3 trigonometrical ratios:

$$\text{Sine of angle} \quad = \quad \frac{\text{Opposite side}}{\text{Hypotenuse}}$$

$$\text{Cosine of angle} \quad = \quad \frac{\text{Adjacent side}}{\text{Hypotenuse}}$$

$$\text{Tangent of angle} \quad = \quad \frac{\text{Opposite side}}{\text{Adjacent side}}$$

These relationships can be remembered by the sentence: '**S**ome **o**f **H**arry's **c**ars **a**re **h**aving **t**rouble **o**n **a**cceleration', in which the first letter of each word are is the first letter of each of these concepts and in the order in which they relate to each other.

SUMMARY

1. Make sure you understand the full range of arithmetical and mathematical symbols which you may encounter.

2. Master the order of arithmetical operations.

3. Learn the quick ways of telling whether a number is a factor of another number.

4. It is a fallacy that working slowly is working carefully. The reverse is true.

5. Use approximations and check your answers in different ways.

6. There is more than one kind of average.

7. Practise translating information from textual to graphic and algebraic forms.

8. Understand the range of diagrammatic techniques for presenting information and also their strengths and weaknesses.

9. Understand how to solve equations.

10. Aim to find the most elegant solutions.

CASE STUDIES

Tom sticks at a certain level

Tom Elliot is not a brilliant mathematician, but he is quite good with figures.

He's a little lazy, though. He doesn't bother to approximate and he doesn't always check his answers. Consequently, he is not all that reliable in his calculations. He can translate between different presentation types – tabular to diagrammatic, algebraic to diagrammatic, and so on – and he can solve simple equations, though he would not be able to solve more complex ones.

Jennifer moves ahead

Jennifer Goss is quite quick with figures and she understands the order of arithmetic operations. Although language based subjects are really her forte, she can translate between different data forms quite easily and can solve equations reasonably well.

Karen feels at sea

Karen Morris becomes bewildered when faced with figures. If she has to deal with them she works slowly, making frequent mistakes. The idea of approximating seems bizarre to her. Ask her to translate from diagrammatic data to tabular or algebraic forms and she will tell you she wouldn't have a clue where to start. As for looking for the most elegant solutions – any solutions at all would be enough for Karen. It is not really her subject.

DISCUSSION POINTS

1. Suggest three ways averages could be used to mislead.

2. Consider some of the ways different diagrammatic techniques could be used to mislead.

3. How important do you think it is to search for elegance in mathematical solutions?

6
Handling Coursework
and Exams

HOW YOU ARE ASSESSED

Methods of assessment vary from one college, faculty or course to another. Some base assessment entirely on exams, others entirely on coursework. Still others base it on a mixture of both coursework and exams in varying proportions.

Preparing coursework

The type of coursework assignments used for assessment will also vary and may include projects, dissertations, or even theses. Exams vary too from college to college, faculty to faculty, and subject to subject. The types of tests found in examinations include:

- essays

- data response tests

- multiple choice questions.

Essays

Essay questions can be of various kinds, and it is important to familiarise yourself with the various types. Descriptive essays often include the word 'Describe' in the question. When the examiner is expecting you to concentrate on explaining something, the question will include the word 'Explain'. Other essay questions will have the word 'Discuss' in them. These questions include a statement, often highly provocative, and ask you to discuss it.

It is vital to understand what is required in discussion questions. Here you are being asked to debate a subject, and so you must get off any personal 'hobby-horse' and look at both sides. A dogmatic answer on a subject you feel strongly about is unlikely to win a high mark when there are good counter arguments you have not looked at.

Example of a 'discussion' essay

Suppose you feel very strongly against the expansion of nuclear power and you are asked to write an essay discussing the issue. You have to stand in the pro-nuclear people's shoes, too and present their arguments, even though those shoes are uncomfortable. To argue only one side of the case is to deny there are any counter arguments being voiced; but you know there are, otherwise it would not be an emotive issue.

You are not being tested on moral values; you are being tested on your academic knowledge and skill. You need to show you can keep the two things detached from each other. Developing the ability to do this will aid your moral cause, anyway, for you will argue your case much better if you understand the thinking of the other side.

We can never completely divorce ourselves from our feelings about a subject, though. As mentioned in the last chapter, it is a mark of intellectual integrity to declare where your personal values lie on an emotional issue (in the introduction) both to acknowledge this limitation in your thinking and to allow the reader to take it into account. The reader is, thus, invited to say to himself, 'This writer has the insight to appreciate that, however much he tries to look at both sides of the coin, his biases will still influence his treatment of the subject. He has been conscientious enough to declare those biases so they are less likely to influence me, the reader, too.' The essay is, thus, a more truly intellectual work. You can get back on your hobby-horse after you have done the exam, but stay loose till then.

Discussion essay techniques

One formula for handling 'discuss' type essays is to begin by defending the statement in the essay question, and then put the case against. Finally, sum up the arguments on both sides and draw a conclusion. This is known as a vertical structure.

Another way to handle this kind of question is to put each argument supporting the statement followed by its counter argument/s in turn. This is a lateral structure and is popular in the social sciences.

'Compare and contrast' essays

Another kind of essay question often found is the 'Compare and contrast' type. In this kind of essay you are being asked to look for both similarities and differences.

How much are you expected to write?

How much are you expected to write in the time allowed? An adult is expected to be able to write about 1,000 words an hour, non-stop. Therefore, after allowing a few minutes' planning time per question (including question selection), you are left with about forty-minutes for the writing. This means you are expected to write around 700 words.

In 700 words you can expect to cover between three and four points substantially. If there are other things you want to include, then comment briefly on them in a paragraph just before the summary. You will never be able to cover everything relevant to a question, least of all in an examination size essay. You can only hope to cover the most important points.

Answering multiple choice questions (MCQs)

Sometimes you will be asked to make one or more choices from a number (usually 5) of alternative answers to a series of questions. There are different types of these, too. They may be any of the following:

- True or false.

- Which is the odd one out?

- Find the matching pair.

- Select the idea represented by the diagram.

- Straight answer type (*eg* which of the following are metals?)

- Which pair of statements are both correct?

- Truth of assertions.

The 'truth of assertions' type needs careful attention. The meanings of the answer options are not as clear as in other types of MCQ. Each has to be read and interpreted carefully. There is often more than one decision to be made in respect of each option. You cannot quickly say, 'This is right' or 'This is wrong'. It is more a case of, 'This is partially right, but is it totally right?'

In the truth/reason type multiple choice questions we first have to work out whether both parts of the statement are correct or not and if they are whether one part expresses the reason why the other part is correct.

Computer-marked assignments

Sometimes multiple choice questions are given in computer-marked assignments (CMAs). Here, instead of circling, or ticking the correct answer, examinees are required to show their answer on a special sheet which will be read by computer. There will be a series of boxes for each question, each one representing a different answer option. Each box contains a broken line and the examinee has to indicate the chosen box by bridging the gap in the broken line in the chosen box. The examination centre's computer can read this and automatically mark the exam paper.

Answering data response questions

There are also **data response type** questions, varying from exam board to exam board. Some take considerable effort to work out; others are more straightforward. Some progress in difficulty, the early parts focussing more on knowledge, the later ones testing understanding and application more.

REACHING YOUR PEAK

You will cover a lot in your course, and also forget a great deal. As mentioned in the last chapter, research has shown that students remember only about a fifth of what they have learned after about two weeks. It is important, therefore, that you begin revising early, in fact from about week 3 of your course. You will even forget some of what you revise, so it is important also to revise what you have revised every month or so.

One method often recommended by educators is to test yourself ten minutes after learning something. The point of highest recall occurs after a lapse of 10-minutes. Patch up the gaps in your knowledge and test yourself again after a day. Following this, repeat the process after a week and then after a month. If you rigorously follow this procedure you will be working pretty efficiently.

Pacing yourself

If we study something very intensively for a long time, we become weary of it. A decline in performance and motivation may follow. The last thing we need is to reach that point just before the exams. Follow the example of champion athletes. They train intensely until a period before the challenge and then ease off for a while, keeping their bodies just ticking over with more moderate exercise.

By the time they enter the crucial race their bodies are raring to go again.

Be a mental athlete: use your head in the same way. Plan your efforts for information intake and skill acquisition – and also revision and 'revision of revision' – so that a week before the exams you are confident of knowing enough to ease the pressure off.

The only way you will achieve this is by planning well in advance. Figure 13 is an example of a revision plan for a one-year course, for example Part One of a bachelor's degree course.

At the start of your course it is important to get a clear idea of what is expected of you by the examiners. Review this regularly to correct for any misconceptions. You assess what is required of you by studying:

- The syllabus
- Past papers
- Classwork
- Homework
- Teachers' comments on essays
- Lecture notes
- The core textbook for the course

QUESTION SPOTTING

Many students overlook the key resource of past exam papers. These should be available in your college library. If you study the last few years' papers you will be surprised at how questions are repeated over the years, often even in the same wording. Questions appearing one year may be missed out the next year, but appear the year after. Sometimes they appear in consecutive years with the wording changed slightly. Go to your library and look up the past papers in week one of your course.

TUTOR-MARKED ASSIGNMENTS (TMAs)

These are essays or projects marked by your teacher and which count towards the overall course grade.

Tutor discretion
Tutors vary in what they look for, in what they give high marks for, and what they penalise. There is always a degree of tutor discretion, but in some courses the degree of discretion is wide.

One Year Revision Plan

Week no.	Current topic	Revision topic
1	Overview	
2	Supply	
3		
4	Demand	Supply
5		
6	Price	Demand
7		
8	Elasticity	Price and Supply
9		
10	Monopoly	Elasticity and Demand
11	Competition	Monopoly and Price
12	Economic systems	Competition and Elasticity
13		
14	Theory of the firm	Economic systems and Monopoly
15		
16	The capital market	Theory of the firm and Competition
17	Geog. distr. of industr.	The capital market and Economic systems
18		
19	Trade unions	Geogr. distr. of industr. and Theory of the firm
20	Money	Trade unions and The capital market
21	Government incm & Expndtr.	Money and Geogr. distr. of industr.
22		
23	Keynesian economic theory	Government income and expenditure and Trade unions
24		
25	Monetarist theory	Keynesian theory and Money
26		
27	International trade	Monetarist theory and Govt. income and expndtr.
28		
29	The multiplier	International trade and Keynesian theory
30	Inflation	The multiplier and Monetarist theory
31		
32	Unemployment	Inflation and International trade
33	Scheduled class-based revision	plus Unemployment and The multiplier
34	"	plus Inflation
35	"	plus unemployment

Fig. 13. What a revision plan for one year of a course could look like.

Some tutors will value opinions highly in essays; others will expect students to keep these to themselves and present only the arguments and evidence in the literature. Some will expect professional quality referencing and bibliographies; others are less concerned about this. Some tutors are strict about word limits and will penalise students who exceed them. Others, however, are quite flexible.

You will learn these guidelines gradually, and perhaps to your cost, as your essays are submitted and returned with sometimes disappointing marks. By the time you have learned what will get you high or low marks you may be changing to a new tutor, whose criteria are to some degree different, and the process starts all over again. It is crucial, therefore, that you talk to your tutor early on and establish the ground rules.

Dual role of TMAs

Remember, TMAs have the dual role of assessment and teaching. Many students regard essay marks and tutors' comments as merely rewards or punishment for effort put in. But by reading this feedback carefully you can make crucial amendments to your approach, and so do better next time. Indeed, that is what tutors' comments are for. Unfortunately, they are often illegible, but if this is so it gives you a good excuse to go and talk to your tutor, at which time you can raise other points and queries you would like to resolve and obtain any other advice you need, besides transcription of his/her illegible comments.

Layout of TMAs

When you submit tutor marked assignments make sure you leave plenty of space.

- Write or type in double spacing.

- Leave a good margin at each side and at the top and bottom of the page to enable the tutor to make his/her comments.

COMPUTER-MARKED ASSIGNMENTS (CMAs)

CMAs are easy to complete. It is just a matter of joining up the break in the line in the option box chosen in a particular question. If you get it wrong, you can effectively cancel the join mark you have made by pencilling in the whole box and then joining the line-break in the box you should have marked. Colouring in the whole box will be read by the computer as if the box had not been touched at all.

Be legible

Whatever type of assessment your course has – 100% coursework, joint coursework/exam work, 100% exam work – your work should always be legible. You will not be given high marks for the right ideas if your examiners or tutors cannot read them.

FINAL EXAM PREPARATION

Your task is to *acquire* knowledge, and skill in *using* that knowledge. The memory techniques discussed in the last section will help you retain what you have learned and skill in using the knowledge can be enhanced by setting yourself mock exams from past papers. A month or so before the exams you need to make yourself a new revision plan. You will, by then, know which areas you need to revise most on and those for which your grasp is firm.

Make a 30-day plan, featuring each hour of the working day, and shade in all your contact time (lectures and tutorial times). Also shade in scheduled social events. What remains is available for revision work.

Ease off in the last week so that you are revising 35 hours at most in that week.

Exam period revision plan

You will probably have class revision scheduled. During these periods take the opportunity of raising with your tutor any outstanding queries, or of clarifying points about which you still have doubts. If there is no class revision scheduled, make an appointment to resolve any such issues with your tutor well before the exam.

Updating your plan

Revision should not cease just because exams have started. You will still need to keep your knowledge and skill in tip-top condition with regular limbering up between exams. It is advisable to make a new revision plan to cover this period, shading in the exam times. The reason a new plan is necessary is that particular subjects will gradually cease to be relevant. Your scheduling of revision periods for each subject will need to take into account the timing of exams

	Mon	Tue	Wed	Thur	Fri	Sat
9.00	B 1	C 2	M 3	B 5	C 6	M 7
10.00	B 2	C 3	M 4	B 6	C 7	M 8
11.00						
12.00	C 1	M 2	B 4	C 5	M 6	B 8
13.00	C 2	M 3	B 5	C 6	M 7	B 9
14.00						
15.00	M 1	B 3	C 4	M 5	B 7	C 8
16.00	M 2	B 4	C 5	M 6	B 8	C 9
17.00						
18.00	B 2	C 3	M 4	B 6	C 7	M 8
19.00	B 3	C 4	M 5	B 7	C 8	M 9
	Mon	Tue	Wed	Thur	Fri	Sat
9.00	B 9	C 10	M 11	B 13	C 14	M 15
10.00	B 10	C 11	M 12	B 14	C 15	M 16
11.00						
12.00	C 9	M 10	B 12	C 13	M 14	B 16
13.00	C 10	M 11	B 13	C 14	M 15	B 17
14.00						
15.00	M 9	B 11	C 12	M 13	B 15	C 16
16.00	M 10	B 12	C 13	M 14	B 16	C 17
17.00						
18.00	B 10	C 11	M 12	B 14	C 15	M 16
19.00	B 11	C 12	M 13	B 15	C 16	M 17
	Mon	Tue	Wed	Thur	Fri	Sat
9.00	B 17	C 18	M 19	B 21	C 22	M 23
10.00	B 18	C 19	M 20	B 22	C 23	M 24
11.00						
12.00	C 17	M 18	B 20	C 21	M 22	B 24
13.00	C 18	M 19	B 21	C 22	M 23	B 25
14.00						
15.00	M 17	B 19	C 20	M 21	B 23	C 24
16.00	M 18	B 20	C 21	M 22	B 24	C 25
17.00						
18.00	B 18	C 19	M 20	B 22	C 23	M 24
19.00	B 19	C 20	M 21	B 23	C 24	M 25
	Mon	Tue	Wed	Thur	Fri	Sat
9.00	B 25	C 26	M 27	B 29	C 30	M 31
10.00	B 26	C 27	M 28	B 30	C 31	M 32
11.00						
12.00	C 25	M 26	B 28	C 29	M 30	B 32
13.00	C 26	M 27	B 29	C 30	M 31	B 33
14.00						
15.00	M 25	B 27	C 28	M 29	B 31	C 32
16.00	M 26	B 28	C 29	M 30	B 32	C 33
17.00						
18.00	B 26	C 27	M 28	B 30	C 31	M 32
19.00	B 27	C 28	M 29	B 31	C 32	M 33

Fig. 14. Example of a 30-day exam revision plan. B = Biology, C = Chemistry, M = Mathematics. The numbers refer to topics.

Week 1

	Mon	Tue	Wed	Thur	Fri	Sat
9.00				EXAM	EXAM	
10.00	BIOL	CHEM	MATH	EXAM	EXAM	
11.00	BIOL	CHEM	MATH	EXAM	EXAM	CHEM
12.00						
13.00	LUNCH	LUNCH	LUNCH	LUNCH	LUNCH	LUNCH
14.00	EXAM	BIOL	BIOL	BIOL	BIOL	BIOL
15.00	EXAM	BIOL	BIOL	BIOL	MATH	BIOL
16.00	EXAM					
17.00		BIOL	CHEM	CHEM	MATH	
18.00						
19.00						

Week 2

	Mon	Tue	Wed	Thur	Fri	Sat
9.00	EXAM		CHEM	EXAM		
10.00	EXAM	BIOL	CHEM	EXAM	MATH	CHEM
11.00	EXAM	BIOL		EXAM	MATH	CHEM
12.00			MATH			
13.00	LUNCH	LUNCH	LUNCH	LUNCH	LUNCH	LUNCH
14.00	BIOL	EXAM	CHEM	EXAM		
15.00	BIOL	EXAM	CHEM	EXAM	CHEM	CHEM
16.00		EXAM		EXAM	CHEM	
17.00			MATH			
18.00	MATH	CHEM			MATH	
19.00	MATH					

Week 3

	Mon	Tue	Wed	Thur	Fri	Sat
9.00	MATH	CHEM	MATH	EXAM		
10.00	MATH	CHEM	MATH	EXAM	MATH	
11.00				EXAM	MATH	
12.00	CHEM	MATH	CHEM			
13.00	LUNCH	LUNCH	LUNCH	LUNCH	LUNCH	
14.00	CHEM	MATH	CHEM		EXAM	
15.00	CHEM	MATH	CHEM		EXAM	
16.00					EXAM	
17.00						
18.00						
19.00						

Fig. 15. Example of a revision plan for use during exam period.

on that subject. There is no point in scheduling biology, physics and chemistry revision more or less evenly over a three-week exam period when all of the chemistry is over by the second week and none of the biology starts until then.

All plans should be reviewed from time to time and re-worked as necessary, as you discover more time is needed for this subject or less for that.

Approaching the exam

As you approach the exam you are likely to become increasingly anxious. This is quite natural. A little anxiety is a good thing when it comes to exams. If it becomes too bad, however, it can sap your energy and reduce your ability to concentrate and grapple with difficult ideas. If this happens, it might be worth talking to someone about it. Universities have educational counselling services. Very few students, however, have this level of difficulty.

Mock exams

It is important that you do at least one mock exam under exam conditions; it is advisable to do many. Only this way will you get some idea of how you will cope in exam conditions and so be able to prepare yourself to overcome any likely difficulties.

The night before

The night before the exam make sure you have everything ready – enough pens, calculator if you need it, ruler and anything else required. Many students take sweets to suck. This is not a bad idea; sweets keep your energy level topped up and perhaps absorb some of the excess energy which would otherwise show itself as anxiety.

The day of the exam

On the day of the exam get up early and have a good breakfast. If your exam is in the morning avoid any further revision. Do not even think about it.

Attempting to cram at this stage may result in driving other ideas away. Exam anxiety will be at its peak, so not only will study be difficult, but may tempt you to give more weight to what you don't know, than to what you do. It is best to leave the material alone now. Let your mind remain in a state of eager readiness, like a horse at the starting gate, full of pent-up energy ready to burst forth when the invigilators utter those words, 'You may start'.

If your exam is in the afternoon it makes sense to limber up with a little light revision during the morning, but give up around twelve o'clock for an exam at half-past two.

Getting there

Leave plenty of time to get to the exam centre. Things can go wrong, buses can be late, cars fail to start. When you arrive, avoid talking to the other candidates. They will be under stress and anxiety is catching. The ingredients of group hysteria are present in the foyer of exam rooms; don't get involved! Keep yourself to yourself and stay in control. Don't forget to go to the loo. You may otherwise waste time for yourself in the exam. Nor is it a simple case of picking up where you left off when you return. It will take a few more valuable minutes to pick up the threads once you get back to your seat.

HANDLING THE EXAM

In the exam room

Enter the exam room as soon as you are allowed and find your seat. Look around. Familiarise yourself with the room. Take some slow deep breaths, expanding the stomach rather than the chest as you inhale. This breathing technique has a calming effect upon the mind and the nervous system.

Get all the things you need organised on your desk and read the exam regulations. Read the front of your exam paper and be ready to start when told. Check you have been given all the supplementary materials, *eg* data booklets in some science exams. If you are supposed to have these it will be stated on the front of the exam paper. It is not unknown for invigilators to forget to give these out; check for yourself.

Reading the questions

Brainstorming

Select which questions to do. Spend four minutes per question brainstorming. Brainstorming is a technique for generating ideas. Just focus your mind on the particular area and jot down everything which comes into it. Don't consider whether the idea is relevant or not at this stage. The process is one of 'free association of ideas'. Ideas enter our heads in random fashion by connecting to ideas which are already there. Using this technique you are getting ideas out in the same way as they went in. As one idea comes to mind a connected idea will follow, and then one connected to that. If you bring selection into it it breaks the free flow. After four minutes you will find you have quite a lot of ideas written down.

Idea selection

Selection comes next. Run quickly through the ideas you have jotted down and mark the most important ones (three or four for a 700-word essay). Mark also those ideas which you feel ought to have a mention, but are not as central as the first ones you picked out. These are ideas which you would like to develop fully if you had more time and space; they can be dealt with in a commentary way in a paragraph just before the summary.

Structuring your ideas

Quickly number your points in the order you will use them in the essay; strike out those you will not be using. Working quickly, draw up an essay plan for each essay, noting the main ideas and the evidence or authorities you will use to support them. This selection and ordering stage should take about one minute per question.

Writing your answers

Before you start an essay, remember to write the number of the question at the top of the page. Doubt about whether they have done this causes many a student needless anxiety after the exam.

Stick to the question

A common mistake is to read a question precisely, and then go on to answer a completely different one. This is very easy to do. You may start out answering exactly what the question asked and suddenly find you have gone off on a tangent. To avoid this, ask yourself not only what the question is asking for, but also what it is *not* asking for, and come up with some answers. Furthermore, briefly state in your introduction how you interpreted the question.

This both communicates to the examiner that you have thought carefully about the question and also defended your interpretation of it. It also helps to ensure that you will not stray off the question and lose marks for doing so. After each paragraph ask yourself, 'Am I still on the point or am I straying off?' Ask yourself also whether the next idea you intend to use will still be on course. Another safeguard is to concentrate on the very words in the question; make sure your answer relates directly to them.

Answer the question in full
Make sure you answer every part of the question, not just the parts which seem more obvious, or for which you have most information.

Introducing your answer
Begin your introductions with an interpretation of the question. Then give a general statement indicating the kind of answer you are going to give and, if relevant, the conclusion you will draw. List the ideas you intend to use; state the order you will use them and the reasoning behind your thinking. If it is a value-charged subject (for example, fox-hunting) state what your personal feelings on the subject are so that the reader may take them into account and give you credit for scholarly integrity.

Be clear
Express your ideas clearly. Use straightforward words and simple sentence structures. Avoid jargon and elaborate style. Write with a particular target-audience in mind. Unless told otherwise, imagine your reader to be an intelligent lay person without special knowledge of the subject, someone able to understand your arguments if you express them clearly.

Be legible
Nobody is going to expect your handwriting to be a work of art, and even the best handwriting will deteriorate when writing non-stop for three hours, but the examiner will have to be able to read it.

Diagrams
Only use diagrams if necessary, for example if asked to do so. If you do, then label them consecutively as you go, for example fig. 1, fig. 2 . . .

Budget your time
Allocate your time in the exam in proportion to the percentage of total marks relating to each part of the paper. Suppose, for example, a three-hour paper has three parts, attracting 60%, 30% and 10% of the total marks, respectively. It would be appropriate to allocate one hour 48 minutes to part one, 54 minutes to part two and 18 minutes to part three. Within the total time allocated for each part of the paper, allocate the time for each question by dividing by the number of questions to be answered. For example,

if three questions were to be answered in part one each question should be allocated about 36 minutes. Organise your time in this way and stick to it rigorously. You will be able to plan in advance by looking at past papers.

However well you may be able to tackle questions like the ones on the exam paper in normal circumstances, under exam conditions your mind will not work quite so efficiently. Two things significantly limit our thinking capacity: stress, and channel overload (simply too much to attend to). In an exam you have both of these. The best approach is to split the task up and do one thing at a time.

Allocate six minutes per question for the planning stage, (including question selection). It is advisable to do all of your planning at once. Some people become alarmed when they look around themselves 15 minutes into the exam and see everyone writing frantically while they are still at the planning stage. Don't be concerned. An hour and a half later you will see the same people biting the end of their pens and staring into space looking for inspiration, while you are writing energetically with a plan which will see you through to the end.

Do your decision-taking first. Select carefully which questions you are going to answer, allowing about four minutes for this in a three-hour paper. Don't make the mistake, as many do, of simply opting for those questions which relate to subjects you know most about. This doesn't mean to say you will be able to give a good answer to that particular question; you have to think about this aspect, too. Sometimes, a question which relates to a subject which is not exactly your best, can still call upon just that portion of knowledge that you have mastered well, and a structure of argument springs readily to mind.

Begin by going over the whole paper. Then go back and select those questions you feel you will be able to give the best answers to. It is important to read each question carefully, they are often slightly misleading.

- Underline what you feel are the key words.

- Bracket off different parts of the question.

- Consider whether you could define the key terms and how well you could deal with each part of the question.

- In a 700 word essay an examiner is likely to be looking for three to four main points. Can you see that many possibilities?

- Mark clearly the questions you are going to do, so that you will not have to run over your thinking each time you move on.

Some students do not realise that they do not have to answer the questions consecutively. You can if you wish begin with question 5 and then go on to question 2, followed by 1 and then 6, for example.

Next, spend four minutes per question brainstorming to generate ideas. Spend a further minute per question selecting the ideas you will use from those you will not and numbering the points as they will appear in the essay. Then get started writing. Be rigorous about time allocation; do not over-run timewise on questions you can answer well. Never, never, leave one question out altogether, for example deciding to answer three questions well instead of four less well. You can never hope to get high marks doing this. It is always better to do a poor answer on a fourth question than to not do it at all. It would be rare for a student to know nothing at all relevant to a particular question. At least make notes of arguments and evidence you would have used in a properly constructed essay. You are likely to get something for these if they are relevant and any limitation of the damage from leaving a question out is better than nothing.

Staying in control

The stress of the exam can even make the obvious seem obscure. However, if you organise your time like this then once you have completed your planning all your mind has to concentrate on is communicating the ideas. Candidates who have jumped straight into writing mode will be searching for ideas, and trying to structure them, as well as working out how to communicate them. This is not an easy task at the best of times, least of all under exam conditions. No wonder mental blocks occur. This way your mind is doing only one thing at a time, and can devote all its attention. Though under greater pressure than normal, its lack of efficiency is made up for by the fact that demands upon it are somewhat reduced.

If you get confused move on to the next question and be prepared to go back to the earlier one later. You do not have to leave pages of space for this. You can continue an essay several pages on after the next question by referencing with the words

'Continued on p___' at the end of one section, and 'Continued from p.___' at the beginning of the next.

Checking your answers

If you write quickly and continuously you will have a few minutes at the end for checking your answers and editing your essays. Scan quickly through your work looking for grammatical and punctuation faults and obvious spelling mistakes. When you are writing that many words there are likely to be some errors.

Use all the pages of your answer book; don't leave blank pages between questions. Use all the time available in the exam. The three-hour time span has been planned to stretch even the best students. If you leave before the end, convincing yourself you didn't need as much time as the examiners set, you will be fooling yourself. There are always things you can do to improve what you've done in the remaining time available.

Common faults
- not defining terms

- not mentioning the principles involved

- not backing up arguments with evidence

- using relevant information but missing the point of the question

- failing to draw conclusions where relevant

- failing to consider whether generalisations can be made

After the exam
Conducting lengthy post-mortems after an exam is bad for you. You will tend to think about what you did not do – what you left out, what you got wrong. This may damage your self-esteem and could lead you to develop a negative attitude towards exams. This doesn't help when you may have to take other exams in the future.

On the other hand, if you don't reflect upon your performance at all you will not learn by your mistakes. The answer is to get the balance right. Reflect on your performance in as detached a way as you can soon after the exam. Consider how you will prevent any errors or weaknesses in performance recurring in a later exam. Remember, the purpose is to learn from mistakes, not to give you reasons to worry for the next few months.

After that forget the exam. Don't dwell on your performance any longer.

SUMMARY

1. Assess what will be needed by studying the syllabus, past exam papers, classwork, homework, teachers' comments on essays, lecture notes and the core textbook for the course.

2. There are all kinds of essay instructions, multiple-choice question and data-response question types with which you should familiarise yourself.

3. Begin revising early and ease off the pressure just before the exam.

4. A month or so before the exams, set yourself an intensive revision plan and set a new one to cover the exam period just before it starts.

5. Do at least one mock exam under as near exam conditions as possible.

6. Schedule your time in the exam to avoid trying to do everything at once.

7. Allocate time according to the marks available for each part of the paper.

8. Interpret the questions carefully and answer every part of them. Keep checking to make sure you are still on course.

9. Never leave a question out, hoping to make up the mark by doing fewer questions better.

10. Check over your paper carefully at the end.

CASE STUDIES

Tom fails to help himself

Tom Elliot has made no serious attempt to estimate the content of the exam papers in advance, save for looking over a few past papers. He has done a mock exam and he has practised the different types of data response and multiple choice questions in class. He has only just begun his revision, a month before the exams.

Tom doesn't really manage his time well in exams, though he doesn't go to pieces either. He does allocate time appropriately, on the basis of percentage of total marks, but he tries to do everything at once and this is not the best way to use the mind under exam conditions. Tom's question interpretation skills are about average. He is aware that questions can be misleading and he tries to avoid falling into this trap, but his failure always to deal with every part of the question lets him down. He has been known to leave an entire question out before now and tends to leave the exam room early if he considers he has finished.

Jennifer keeps control

Jennifer Goss has taken pains to assess and reassess how the final exams will be pitched. She has carefully compared the classwork, homework, lecture notes, essay questions, teachers' comments on the latter, the course textbook and past exam papers, trying to establish where they overlap. This, she predicts, will more or less be the content of the exams.

She has practised every type of essay question – multiple choice and data response questions. She began revision after the first month of the course and has been systematically doing so ever since. She is now in a position where she can ease off in the run up to the exams. She has set herself a realistic pre-exam revision timetable and will set another plan just before the exams start. She has already done three mock exams under rigid conditions.

Jennifer has no illusions about the limitations of the mind under exam conditions. She plans her time carefully so that she avoids doing everything at once. She allocates time to parts of the paper according to the percentage of total marks.

She interprets the questions very carefully, mistrusting her own interpretations if they seem too straightforward. She knows it is easy to go off course, so she keeps checking each time she finishes a paragraph and prepares to begin a new one. Jennifer would never dream of leaving a question out altogether. She always checks her paper and always finds a few errors to correct.

Karen goes to pieces

Karen Morris goes to pieces in the run-up to exams and almost falls apart in them. She has never got down to predicting the content of the exams, so that she can guide her studies towards them. She has done the multiple choice and data response practice set by her teacher during the year, and has tried one mock exam paper. She has read over her notes a few times during the year, but after a while they became just words. Karen has now set herself a pre-exam revision timetable, but the problem is her revision will be 'just more of the same' – reading and re-reading the words.

Karen does not schedule her time well in exams. She means to but when it comes to the crunch, she looks around and sees everybody writing and so she just 'dives in' too. She sets herself definite times for each question, based on percentage of total marks, but she doesn't stick to them. Her question interpretation is very superficial and so she falls into every trap there is.

DISCUSSION POINTS

1. What are the pros and cons of question spotting (studying past papers)?

2. What would be the benefits to you of doing mock exams?

3. Consider the relative values of each of the various sources for predicting exam content. Are some of them better than others?

Further Reading

GENERAL STUDY SKILLS

Ashman, S, and George A, *Study and Learn* (Heinemann, 1982).
Barnes, R, *Successful Study for Degrees* (Routledge, 1992).
Dunleavy, P, *Studying for a Degree – in the Humanities and Social Sciences* (Macmillan, 1986).
Freeman, R, *Mastering Study Skills* (Macmillan, 1982).
Marshall, L, and Rowland, F, *Guide to Learning Independently* (OU Press, 1993).
Northedge, A, *Good Study Guide* (OU Press, 1990).
Rowntree, D, *Learn How to Study* (Macdonald, 1976).

THINKING SKILLS

Ansell, Gwen, *Make the Most of Your Memory* (National Extension College, 1984).
Buzan, Tony, *Use Your Head* (BBC Books, 1989 edition). The author invented the idea of mind maps.
Jones, Bill and Johnson, Roy, *Making the Grade: A Study Programme for Adult Students. Vol. 1: Reading and Learning: Vol. 2: Thinking and Writing* (Manchester University Press, 1990).
Edwards, Betty, *Drawing on the Right Side of the Brain* (Souvenir Press, 1981).
Fairbairn, G, and Winch, C, *Reading, Writing and Reasoning: A Guide for Students* (Open University Press, 1991).

DOING RESEARCH

Berry, Ralph, *How to Write a Research Paper* (Pergamon Press, 2nd edition 1986).
Hoffman, Ann, *Research For Writers* (A & C Black, 1979).
Todd, Alden, *Finding Facts Fast* (Penguin Books, 1990).

Turabain, Kate I, *A Manual For Writers of Research Papers, Theses and Dissertations* (1982).

WRITING SKILLS

Bowden, John, *How to Write a Report* (How To Books, 2nd edition 1994).

Hennessy, B, *How to Write an Essay* (How To Books, 2nd edition 1995).

Morison, Murray, and Pey, Jim, *Writing Sociology Essays: A Guide for A Level Students* (Longman, 1985).

Pirie, David, *How to Write Critical Essays* (Methuen, 1985).

Smith, Pauline, *How to Write an Assignment* (How To Books, 1994).

Watson, George, *Writing a Thesis* (Longman, 1987).

Whale, John, *Put it in Writing* (Dent, 1984).

EXAMINATIONS

Acres, David, *How to Pass Exams Without Anxiety* (How To Books, 4th edition 1995).

Cocker, D. *Successful Examination Technique* (Northcote House, 1987).

Locke, Dr. *Overcoming Examination Nerves: Successful Studying.* Therapeutic Visualisation Ltd, 6 Milton Road, Bentley Heath B93 8AA.

DICTIONARIES AND REFERENCE BOOKS

Gowers, Sir Ernest, *The Complete Plain Words.* Revised by Sir Bruce Fraser. (Penguin 1977).

The New Collins Thesaurus.

Oxford English Dictionary (OUP).

Oxford Reference Dictionary (OUP).

Phythian, B.A., *Teach Yourself Correct English* (Hodder and Stoughton, 1985).

Roget's Thesaurus. A classic, available in numerous editions.

REVISION AIDS

Letts Study Guides: GCSE, A/AS Level.

Longman Revise Guides, GCSE and A Level.

Longman GCSE Pass Packs.

Glossary

British National Bibliography. A source of information on all books in print in the United Kingdom.

Circadian rhythm. A cyclical pattern of energy levels corresponding to times of the day.

Citation. A reference to the ideas or claims of another writer.

Close reading. Careful reading of part of a text to extract the meaning.

Computer marked assignment (CMA). An assignment designed to be marked automatically by computer. Question papers are completed by making marks which a computer is able to read.

Continuous assessment. An alternative assessment method to that based entirely on final exams. Where continuous assessment is concerned, a student's work will be continuously monitored and assessed. Often, courses are based partly on continuous assessment and partly on finals.

Convergent thinking. Progressively narrowing the range of opinions to arrive at a solution to a problem. Algebra is an example of this problem solving technique. (Contrast with divergent thinking.)

Copyright. The ownership of the sole right to the use of particular literary, musical or visual forms, based on first usage.

Criterion referencing. An assessment method based on objective criteria. (Contrast this with **norm referencing**).

Data response questions. A method of assessment of actual ability to use knowledge in a practical way.

Dewey Decimal System. The common method of library arrangement, based on progressive sub-categorisation of books in orders of ten.

Dissertation. A piece of written work of around 10,000 words.

Divergent thinking. A method of problem solving by widening the system boundary. (Contrast this with convergent thinking).

ELF radiation. Extra low frequency energy emitted from electronic equipment such as VDU screens.

Essay. A piece of written work of significantly less than 10,000 words. Typically, university essays are between 1,500 and 3,000 words.

Gestalt processing. Processing information in a spatial or holistic way, rather than a sequential way. The right hemisphere of the brain is the domain of Gestalt processing and the studygram or spidergram is a graphic representation of this kind of process, in contrast to an algorithm of an essay, which is representative of more left-hemisphere functioning.

Graph. A pictorial representation of a trend.

Hemisphericity. The ability or tendency to utilise one side of the brain relative to the other.

Implicit theme paragraphic style. A style of paragraph construction in which the meaning the writer intends will become apparent to the reader gradually, as he/she reads through the paragraph. Contrast this with the **topic sentence paragraphic style**.

Index. A list of ideas referenced to locations in which they are referred to in a book.

Invigilator. An administrator of an examination. The invigilator ensures the examination runs smoothly and that the rules are strictly adhered to.

Jargon. Esoteric language, ie language which is meaningful only to those who are familiar and well practised in the subject.

Lateral essay structure. An essay structural style in which idea and counter-idea are juxtaposed throughout. Contrast with **vertical style**.

Law. A relationship between two or more variables which holds true in every case.

Lecture. A teaching technique where an expert delivers a prepared speech to an audience. Although there are exceptions, this teaching method is virtually non-interactive; the information flow is one way only. Typically, content tends to be: important and difficult points of information, literary sources and general guidance.

Method of Loci. A memory technique originally used by the ancient Greeks for remembering the structures of their lectures. It involves mentally associating ideas to particular rooms in buildings. The sophists (itinerant teachers) would wander through buildings and memorise the sequence of rooms they entered. The points in the lectures they intended to give would then deliberately be associated in their minds with the different rooms, in accordance with the sequence they were to follow and the sequence in which they had arrived at particular rooms. They would then mentally walk through the buildings as they gave their lectures.

Microfiche. A record of something printed on a small acetate sheet to be viewed in a microfiche reader. Typically, records of books available in a library are of this type.

Mnemonics. Memory techniques.

Mock exam. A dummy-run of an exam, to inform a student of his/her strengths and weaknesses, before the real exam.

Model answers. Typical answers to specimen exam questions, which would be expected to attract high marks.

Multiple choice questions. A form of assessment wherein a student is required to choose from a range of alternative answer options.

Norm referencing. A method of assessment based on the quality of a student's work relative to that of other students. (Contrast this with **criterion referencing**.

Opinion. A personal interpretation of facts not supported by evidence.

Pie chart. The pictorial representation of an idea designed to demonstrate proportionality. It is called a pie chart because it resembles a pie cut into slices.

Pictogram. A graphical method of representing information, involving pictures instead of text or line graphs.

Plagiarism. Breaching intellectual property rights by using an idea first published by another without attributing it to that person in the text. The first publisher of an idea receives intellectual property rights over their ideas. Subsequent users must acknowledge those rights by attributing the idea to that person if they use it.

Quotation. A form in which authority for an idea is presented in a piece of written work by quoting the very words of an acclaimed expert.

Reading list. A list given to students at the start of a course, or part of a course, prescribing the reading they should do.

Redundancy. Excessive references to an idea over and above what is necessary to communicate it, or excessive usage of words in a sentence.

Review of the literature. A presentation regarding the current state of knowledge in a particular area, the purpose of which is to (a) couch the main thesis of the writer's work, and (b) demonstrate the writer's thorough knowledge of the area he/she is contributing to.

Scanning. Swift screening of text to identify relevant parts.

Sequential processing. Processing information in a sequential, logical way, one step at a time. Contrast this with **Gestalt processing**.

Skimming. Glancing through text to develop a general idea of the content.

Studygram. Sometimes called a spidergram, because of its appearance, it is a means of representing ideas on paper in a spatial (rather than sequential) way, with connecting lines drawn between the various parts of the idea.

Synthesis. The bringing together of elements of an analysis to form a meaningful idea.

Seminar. It may be misleading to say what a seminar is in theory and more useful to say what it is in practice, for seminars take various forms depending on the tutor's preference. At the extremes they can amount to discussion between students with the tutor doing little more than observing; on the other hand they can amount to mini-lectures, in which the students do little other than listen and take notes. Their form lies somewhere between these two, involving group discussion, teaching, clarification and student presentations.

Topic sentence paragraphic style. A style of paragraph construction in which the main point is stated in the first sentence.

Vertical essay structure. An essay structural style in which the complete 'case for' a position is given before the 'case against', followed by a summary and conclusions.

Index

Abbreviations, 83
Abscissa, 105
Abstracts, 59, 60
Acronyms, 113
Actual self-concept, 19
Algorithms, 112
Anti-glare screen filters, 34
Antonyms, 85
Arithmetic, 100, 101, 104
Averages, 94

Bar chart, 109, 110
Bibliographies, 59, 60, 83, 88, 89, 121
Brackets, 83, 97, 100, 110
Brainstorming, 55, 112, 126, 130
British National Bibliography, 59

Card index systems, 40, 58
Channel overload, 18, 24, 129
Channel capacity, 24
Charts, 46, 66, 94, 105, 109, 110, 112
Classwork, 55, 57, 119
Coltheart's test, 11
Comprehension, 51, 55, 61
Compulsive regression, 62
Computer, 10, 12, 33, 34, 36, 38, 40, 47, 58, 61, 87, 117, 118, 121
Computer marked assignments,

117, 121
Constructive criticism, 23
Contingency plans, 32
Continuous assessment, 44
Coursework, 48, 115
Cramming, 27, 51
Creativity, 13
Cube, 99
Cubic root, 99
Cut and paste, 38

Decimals, 94, 96, 103
Denominator, 100, 101, 103, 110
Dependent variable, 106
Descriptive essays, 82, 85, 115
Dewey decimal system, 58
Dictionaries, 33, 38, 39, 59, 68, 85
Discouragement, 23

Editing, 45, 131
Elegance, 112
ELF and VLF radiation, 36
Encyclopaedias, 39, 59
Energy peak, 45
Equations, 94, 106, 110
Equipment, 34, 37, 41
Essay/s, 38, 40, 44, 45, 48, 51, 53, 62, 63, 71, 72, 82, 84, 85, 87, 91, 93, 115, 116, 118, 119, 121, 127, 130, 131
Exams, 32, 43, 45, 115, 118,

119, 122, 124, 126, 131
Exercise, 46, 47, 80, 118
Experimental attitudes, 27

Factors, 12, 49
Family background influences, 12
Filing, 39, 41
Flash card, 12
Fractions, 87, 94, 100, 101, 110
Furniture, 37

Game playing, 17, 27
General principles, 26
Grammar, 93
Grammar checkers, 38
Graphs, 66, 94, 105, 106
Group dynamics, 55

Handbooks, 32, 39, 52, 53
Handwriting, 21, 86, 128
Hemispherical biases, 11, 12
Homework, 43, 118

Ideal self-concept, 19
Implicit theme styles, 85
Independent variable, 106
Indices, 59, 60, 98, 99
Intellectual property, 89
Intelligence, 12, 14, 83
Intelligent scepticism, 35
Inter-library loans, 58
Interpretation, 81, 127, 128

Jargon, 128
Journals, 59, 60

Lateral structure, 82, 116
Learned hopelessness, 19
Learning objectives, 24
Lecturers, 55, 58
Lectures, 44, 48, 51, 53, 57, 122

Left-brain ability, 12, 112
Libraries, 33, 39, 43, 45, 57, 60, 86
Listening skills, 54
Lowest common multiple, 101, 110

Mathematics, 43, 98
Mean, 104, 105
Median, 104, 105
Memory techniques, 122
Mental fatigue, 18, 34, 35, 47
Microfiches, 58
Microfilm, 59
Mistakes, 14, 27, 131
Mnemonics, 27, 113
Mock exams, 122, 125
Mode, 54, 62, 104, 112, 130
Multiple choice questions, 115, 117, 118
Multiplication tables, 25, 27, 100

Natural rhythms, 41, 42
Neural connections, 27
Newspapers, 59
Noise background, 34
Non-verbal material, 66
Note-taking, 54, 55
Numerator, 100, 102

OK4R method, 69
One-channel processor, 14
Order of arithmetic operations, 100
Order of magnitude, 96
Organisational aids, 32
Overload, 14, 18, 24, 129

Paragraphs, 18, 50, 64, 70, 85, 88, 93
Past papers, 118, 129

Percentages, 94, 103
Periodicals, 59, 60
Persistent errors, 27
Persistent hesitation, 22
Physical comfort, 35
Pictograms, 66, 105, 110
Pictures, 61, 66, 110
Pie charts, 109
Plagiarism, 82
Planning, 22, 31, 32, 44, 46, 117, 119, 129, 130
Plateaux, 22
Play, 12, 17, 23, 27, 46
Point of highest recall, 23, 118
Prefixes, 68
Private tuition, 48
Problem solving, 12, 18, 94, 111, 113
Projects, 44, 46, 48, 55, 115, 119
Punctuation, 51, 83, 90, 131

Quantitative information, 94, 109
Questioning technique, 62

Range, 22, 36, 38, 39, 41, 56, 57, 105
Reading, 14, 26, 33, 37, 42, 47, 51, 52, 54, 56, 58, 60, 63, 67, 69, 70, 73, 121
Reading, lists, 58
skill, 60, 62
speed, 14, 51, 61, 63, 69
Reciprocal, 98, 99
Redundancy control, 35
Referencing, 81, 83, 88, 89, 121, 130
Repetitive strain injury, 36, 47
Researching, 45
Rest, 46, 47, 72
Retention, 79
Revision, 119, 124, 126

Revision plan, 117, 119, 120, 124
Revision time-table, 45
Right-brain styles of thinking, 11, 12
Right-hemisphere, 42
Role-models, 19

Screen glare, 36
Self confidence, 53
Self esteem, 17, 27, 41, 47, 131
Sentences, 64, 65, 70, 83, 85, 88, 93
Sequential processing, 11, 43
Shorthand, 54
Signposts, 64, 71
Software, 38, 61
Sounding board, 9
Spatial ability, 12
Spectacles, 36
Speed of processing, 14
Speed writing, 54
Spell checkers, 38, 45
Spelling, 131
Square, 99, 108
Square root, 99
SQ3R method, 69
Standard deviation, 105
Stationery, 37, 38
Statistics, 11, 54, 66, 94
Study habits, 22
Suffixes, 68
Syllabus, 39, 44, 48, 52, 118
Symbols, 95, 100
Synonyms, 85

Tape recorders, 38
Target audience, 128
Task commitment, 13
Teacher expectations, 51
Temperature, 34, 41, 42
Thesaurus, 33, 38, 39, 85

Thinking style, 9, 11, 12, 20, 112
Time management aids, 41, 46, 50
Topic sentence styles, 65, 70, 85
Trace-decay, 14, 18
Trend lines, 67, 106, 108
Trigonometrical ratios, 113
Tutors, 48, 52, 53, 55, 56, 80, 81, 86, 88, 119, 121, 122, 124
Tutorials, 56, 57, 122

Variables, 66, 106, 112
VDU, 34, 36
Vertical structure, 82, 116
Vocabulary, 51, 62, 67, 68

Word·building, 12
Word count, 87
Word limit, 86, 87, 121
Word processors, 33
Wordspan, 61, 62